REVELS STUDENT EDITIONS

THE DUCHESS OF MALFI
John Webster

Manchester University Press

REVELS STUDENT EDITIONS

Based on the highly respected Revels Plays, which provide a wide range
of scholarly critical editions of plays by Shakespeare's contemporaries,
the Revels Student Editions offer readable and competitively priced
introductions, text and commentary designed to distil the erudition and
insights of the Revels Plays, while focusing on matters of clarity and
interpretation. These editions are aimed at undergraduates, graduate
teachers of Renaissance drama and all those who enjoy the vitality and
humour of one of the world's greatest periods of drama.

GENERAL EDITOR David Bevington

Dekker/Rowley/Ford *The Witch of Edmonton*
Fletcher *The Tamer Tamed; or, The Woman's Prize*
Ford *'Tis Pity She's a Whore*
Jonson *Bartholomew Fair*
Jonson *Volpone*
Jonson *Masques of Difference: Four Court Masques*
Kyd *The Spanish Tragedy*
Marlowe *The Jew of Malta*
Marlowe *Tamburlaine the Great*
Marston *The Malcontent*
Middleton *Women Beware Women*
Middleton/Rowley *The Changeling*
Middleton/Tourneur *The Revenger's Tragedy*
Webster *The Duchess of Malfi*
Webster *The White Devil*

Plays on Women: An Anthology
Middleton *A Chaste Maid in Cheapside*
Middleton/Dekker *The Roaring Girl*
Anon. *Arden of Faversham*
Heywood *A Woman Killed with Kindness*

REVELS STUDENT EDITIONS

THE DUCHESS OF MALFI

John Webster

Edited by John Russell Brown

based on The Revels Plays edition
edited by John Russell Brown
published by Methuen & Co., 1964
and by Manchester University Press, 1977

MANCHESTER
UNIVERSITY PRESS

Manchester and New York

distributed in the United States exclusively by
Palgrave Macmillan

Introduction, critical apparatus, etc.
© John Russell Brown 1997

The right of John Russell Brown to be identified as the editor of this work
has been asserted by him in accordance with the Copyright, Designs and
Patents Act 1988.

Published by Manchester University Press
Oxford Road, Manchester M13 9NR, UK
and Room 400, 175 Fifth Avenue, New York, NY 10010, USA

www.manchesteruniversitypress.co.uk

Distributed in the United States exclusively by
Palgrave Macmillan, 175 Fifth Avenue, New York,
NY 10010, USA

Distributed in Canada exclusively by
UBC Press, University of British Columbia, 2029 West Mall,
Vancouver, BC, Canada V6T 1Z2

British Library Cataloguing-in-Publication Data
A catalogue record for this book is available from the British Library

Library of Congress Cataloging-in-Publication Data applied for

ISBN 978 0 7190 4357 4 *paperback*

First published 1997

16 15 14 13 12 11 10 09 08   12 11 10 9 8 7 6

Printed in Great Britain
by Bell & Bain Ltd, Glasgow

Preface

I have been glad of the opportunity to re-work my Revels Plays edition of *The Duchess of Malfi* which was first published in 1964. In almost every way this is a new edition, reflecting a new view of the play. Since completing that Revels edition, I have learnt a great deal about the play from others and I am most appreciative and grateful for their help. Colleagues and students, in particular at the Universities of Sussex and Michigan, have both encouraged and informed me. The increasing number of productions and editions of the play and many of the publications about Webster in general have also contributed; the sections on Stage History and Further Reading in my introduction can give only such a brief account of this as space allows.

I am particularly indebted to two special occasions. The first was an invitation to lead a seminar at the Folger Library Institute which allowed me to return to that great and accessible collection. The second was an invitiation to lecture on Webster at the University of Otago, New Zealand, which provided the spur for me to reconsider this play in the light of recent scholarship and criticism and of my own experience of it in the theatre.

My greatest thanks, and deepest, are to the General Editor of this new Revels Student Edition of Renaissance plays. Not only did he give scrupulous attention to my submissions, but also caused me to think again about many of the decisions I had made to the great improvement of what is now presented to readers. This work is much the better for David Bevington's learning and generous contributions. The faults remaining are very much my own responsibility.

John Russell Brown
Court Lodge, Hooe
7 June 1996

Introduction

In 1944 Joseph Brearley arrived as the new English teacher at Hackney Downs Grammar School in London and soon fired his pupils with enthusiasm for Shakespeare. At the age of fifteen, Harold Pinter played Macbeth in the school's first drama production, and forty years later, in an article in *The Times* (London, 18 March 1995), the dramatist declared that 'Shakespeare dominated our lives at that time.' But outweighing that, 'the revelation which Joe Brearley brought with him was John Webster ... On our walks, we would declare into the wind, at the passing trolley buses or indeed to the passers-by, nuggets of Webster.' In *The Duchess of Malfi*, for example, he had found the cryptic, burdened, undeniably memorable, and startlingly dramatic: 'Cover her face; mine eyes dazzle; she died young' (IV.ii.263). Years afterwards he remembered: 'That language made me dizzy'.

Perhaps, in those postwar years, the hold that Webster can take over his readers was felt by comparatively few people, but by the mid-1990s that had changed. One production of *The Duchess of Malfi*, using the simplest of sets, toured for months around the world and played to capacity houses in London at a West End theatre and, in the same theatre and the same season, only a few months previously, another production of the same play, with a more elaborate set but a very small cast, had settled in for an extended run. Declan Donnellan, director of the later of these two stagings, declared that the Duchess is: 'a tragic figure who ... outmatches Cleopatra or Lady Macbeth in the depth as well as the extremity of her suffering ... She has to lose her vanity, shed her self-protective identity, and try to discover who she really is, like Oedipus or King Lear or Richard II' (interview in *The Times*, London, 29 December 1995).

The Duchess of Malfi can provoke many different reactions, most of them extreme. In 1960 Kenneth Tynan had quoted G. H. Lewes, another theatre critic writing a hundred years earlier, to second his own condemnation of Webster's tragedy for 'the irredeemable mediocrity of its dramatic evolution of human passion'. Disapproval

1

has often been more confident than its opposite, but by the 1990s Webster's reputation had become more secure. The texts were now widely available in editions that were more or less up-to-date in scholarship and aware of the play's theatrical vitality. The two tragedies which are his unique masterpieces could be seen in performance with growing frequency, and not only in English-speaking theatres. Small touring or 'experimental' companies, and student theatres, staged them even more often: Declan Donnellan had been Duke Ferdinand twenty years earlier as an undergraduate actor. Webster was gaining audiences as well as readers, and his reputation soared in consequence.

Among changing tastes however, one reaction has been a constant. His contemporaries, both in praise and satire, considered Webster's style to be 'industrious', and, in writing about his own work in prefaces to published texts, the author only encouraged this assessment. It is undeniable; and, down the centuries, whenever Webster's dazzling eloquence or profound feeling and understanding has been acclaimed, his painstaking artifice or vigilant carefulness is usually acknowledged with the next breath.

ORIGINS, CONTEXT, AND COMPOSITION

After years of working in collaboration with other dramatists, at the age of thirty-two or thereabouts, married, and with young children, John Webster completed his first unaided play, *The White Devil*. He had used a large and miscellaneous collection of sources, piecing together his own stage version of real-life happenings in Italy some thirty years previously. He left little as he found it, changing the course and outcome of the story and adding snippets of information, mixed with gossip and fantasy, and also drawing upon his own reading of prose, verse, and drama, and on his intimate knowledge of the London stage and of London life. The resultant tragedy was both complex and sensational. In a preface to its publication in 1612, he defended himself against those who reported that he had been 'a long time in finishing this tragedy'. Acknowledging his ambition, he retorted that he did not write with 'a goose-quill, winged with two feathers'; and reminded his readers that Euripides, when criticized for taking three days to write three lines, had defended himself by saying they would continue to be read for 'three ages'.

The White Devil had its first performance early in 1612, and *The Tragedy of the Duchess of Malfi* was then completed, with much less delay, by the spring or autumn of 1614, or late the previous year. It was performed not among the frankly popular shows of the Queen's Men at the Red Bull Theatre as his first tragedy had been but by the King's Men at the indoors Blackfriars Theatre within the city walls and at the newly rebuilt Globe Theatre on the South Bank of the River Thames. This company was the most prestigious in the land, playing frequently at court and drawing such an audience to the Blackfriars that neighbours complained that the streets were choked with coaches bearing important persons to the plays. This more intimate theatre had been used by the King's Men only since 1610 or 1611, and yet from the start the actors had been able to charge substantially more for admission; the cheapest price was sixpence for a seat, rather than the one penny paid by the notorious 'stinkards' for standing in the yards of the 'public' playhouses. The King's Men were also developing a newer, post-Shakespearian style of drama; while their leading playwright had written little after 1611 and then only in collaboration, they had found two new and prolific writers, John Fletcher, fifteen years Shakespeare's junior and son of a well-connected clergyman who was briefly Bishop of London, and Francis Beaumont, younger by another five years, a part-time lawyer and a country gentleman.

Newly accepted among this company and working for its two theatres, Webster chose to dramatize the story of the Duchess of Malfi as told by William Painter in *The Palace of Pleasure*. This story was not new and had been taken originally from real life. In 1490, at twelve years old, Giovanna d'Aragona had been married to the Duke of Amalfi; at nineteen or twenty, she was left a widow; and then, after about five years, she fell in love with her chief steward, Antonio Bologna, and married him. She realized that making a low-born servant her husband would outrage and anger her two brothers, the elder a cardinal and the younger inheriting the family's title. She therefore kept the relationship secret until rumours of a second childbirth reached them, when, to avoid trouble, her husband went into exile and she soon followed. Deserted by servants and pursued by her brothers, the young family took refuge in Ancona until the Cardinal arranged that the papal Legate should banish Antonio. They then fled to Sienna, where again the Cardinal persuaded the city authorities to banish Antonio. As the family were leaving this refuge, they were intercepted by soldiers who took the mother and two children to Milan. After that, nothing more was heard of either the Duchess or the babies. Antonio had escaped with their eldest

child, a boy of about six years, only to be assassinated in October of
the following year, 1513. Matteo Bandello told this story in his
Novelle of 1554 and his account was subsequently translated into
French, and also augmented and moralized, by François de
Belleforest in the second volume of his *Histoires Tragiques* (1565).
From this version Painter had taken the tale and published his
translation in 1567, adding his own observations on its events.

Having found the story, Webster, whose habit of research had led
him to numerous sources for his earlier play, was soon in action
again. He consulted both the first edition of *The Palace of Pleasure*
and the second that had followed eight years later, as echoes of both
in the play's dialogue prove. Moreover he was always changing
details of the story, adding characters, inventing incidents of madness, torture, intrigue, insecurity, devotion, ambition, and sexual
encounter, elaborating minor characters, providing five more
corpses in the last Act, bringing the Duchess back to life after she has
been left for dead, and having her speak yet again as an echo from
her grave. He changed names by taking some out of their context,
inventing others, contriving to avoid using any name for the Duchess or her cardinal brother, and changing that of the other brother.
Most importantly, he reconsidered and re-imagined the motives of
all the principal persons involved so that, in his play, they seem to
change before the eyes of the audience as their guards drop or as
danger reveals new resources of mind or feeling.

The story remained much the same in outline, and often Painter's
very words became part of the play's dialogue, but in myriads of
small, as well as more fundamental, ways, every element is made to
serve Webster's own purposes. At the very start one addition marks
his intentions unmistakably. Antonio has returned from France and
his friend Delio is there to mark this moment for the audience by
asking, 'How do like the French court?' (I.i.4). But more is achieved
than that: in Antonio's answer, Webster quotes and adapts a passage
from Sir Thomas Elyot's *Image of Governance* (1541), to the effect
that a king's court should be purged of all vice so that it could be an
example to the entire country. This comment reflects on the action
that is to follow, for immediately Bosola, the 'only court gall', enters
and speaks of corruption in high places and implicates the Cardinal
in covert crime and machination. Webster has invented this
question-and-answer sequence to define his characters in relation to
each other and to ideas about power and religion, private and public
life, the past and the future. And still more is achieved by this

insertion because Webster adds to the argument he found in Elyot by introducing a further issue of great topical concern. He has Antonio refer to the prolonged and increasingly difficult stand-off between King James I and the House of Commons in the London Parliament:

> And what is 't makes this blessèd government
> But a most provident council, who dare freely
> Inform him the corruption of the times?
> Though some o'th' court hold it presumption
> To instruct princes what they ought to do,
> It is a noble duty to inform them
> What they ought to foresee.   (I.i.16–22)

Instruct and *inform*, *duty* and *corruption*: these were the very words with which the Commons insisted that they had the right to tell James how he should rule the country and conduct the affairs of his court. They were not thanked for their *presumption*, and yet they were speaking of differences that within comparatively few years would lead the country back again towards civil war.

This long speech (I.i.4–22) at the head of the play is by no means necessary to its narrative, and sits oddly in the mouth of Antonio, a steward who has no personal involvement in politics at this point in the story. Webster has used it to nail his play to the affairs of England in his own time, and it is only the first in a series of alterations whereby he makes events and characters in Italy at the beginning of the previous century relevant to the lives and concerns of his audience. As in *The White Devil*, the foreign subject-matter allows representation of matters which, if shown within an English or contemporary setting, would have had the play banned and its author imprisoned.

Webster's earlier tragedy had reflected the behaviour of ambitious and ruthless persons at the court of King James; *The Duchess* gives a closer view and shows how King James himself conducted public business and governed the land. With a central character who had lived long ago and in another country, and was a young woman, the author could always disclaim any such intention, but the way in which his Duchess keeps secret her marriage to a low-born member of her household and so places herself at the mercy of other servants had some resemblances to James's behaviour following his attachment to a sequence of handsome young men in his entourage and the ennoblement of some of them. No one would equate the shambling figure of the English king with the appearance of a young widow admired for both beauty and intelligence, but secret meetings, avowals of love to ambitious persons, covert personal meanings in public speeches, domestic intimacies behind closed doors, spying for information about powerful persons, whispering at a distance, dangerous silences, sudden and disproportionate laughter, talk of witchcraft—all these belonged to the time and place of the court in Webster's London. Imprisonment and murder were not unknown there, as Webster had learnt at first hand: in 1613 he had dedicated his *Monumental Column* to Robert Carr, then Viscount Rochester and the object of one of the King's most scandalous infatuations; in April of the same year, Thomas Overbury, Carr's secretary, was imprisoned in the Tower of London where he died shortly afterwards, probably poisoned by the Countess of Essex, who after a sensational divorce would marry Carr.

Webster alters his sources so that the old story becomes in his play a representation of the court, its secrets and dangerous 'ice-pavements' (V.ii.332), its pleasures, pastimes, rumours, and guilty consciences, and the low-born's relentless 'quest of greatness' (V.iv.64). His most obvious devices for bringing such issues into focus are the soliloquy and the dying speech in which a character can at last speak freely. But at least as important is the setting-up of a series of reflective theatre-images, so that one person is always being defined by another, one moment in the play by another. Here Webster's manipulation of his source is highly inventive, original, and continuous.

NARRATIVE, STRUCTURE, AND CHARACTERS

In *The Palace of Pleasure*, Bosola is a 'bloody beast' hired after the death of the Duchess to kill off her husband, Antonio. Webster, however, has him appear in the very first scene as an embittered outsider who is hired by Duke Ferdinand at his brother's suggestion to spy on their sister. He also has Ferdinand ask the Duchess to make him Provisor of the Horse—the manager of her stables—and so a member of the household with easy access to the princely presence. One effect is to set up illuminating similarities and differences between Bosola and Antonio: both are ambitious men without noble blood, and both are advanced, one because of his ruthlessness and reputation for melancholy, the other for sexual attractiveness and, it seems, personal worthiness. These two are several times brought alone together, vying with each other in talk about promotion and influence (see I.i.47–68; II.i.79–111; II.iii.9–52; V.iv.42–84); and both are profoundly affected and, subsequently, destroyed through contact with the Duchess.

Early in the story, Antonio is privately boastful about his wife and family (see his talk with Delio at the beginning of Act II) but, once the marriage is public knowledge, he becomes progressively self-concerned. Fearful for himself, he leaves his wife to the mercy of their enemies, not considering her predicament: 'My heart is turned to a heavy lump of lead, / With which I sound my danger. Fare you well' (III.v.91–2). Bosola is at hand to mark what is happening:

> This proclaims your breeding.
> Every small thing draws a base mind to fear
> As the adamant draws iron.   (III.v.52–4)

After his wife's death, Antonio returns ignominiously to seek money from the Cardinal, who has banished the family from Loretto. Antonio is killed accidentally in the dark by Bosola.

In contrast, Bosola becomes more and more drawn to the mistress he had set out to betray. Here a whole new story is introduced into the play. As 'intelligencer', he tells Ferdinand of the first birth, while failing to recognize that Antonio is the husband (so far beneath the Duchess's attention he considers her steward to be). In the third Act, years later, he gets a false key to her bed-chamber so that Ferdinand can confront his sister and her lover but, when the entire household is roused in alarm, he pretends to such great admiration of Antonio that he wins the heartfelt confidence of the Duchess. From this moment on she is a hunted person, and Bosola takes an active part in that pursuit and her subsequent imprisonment. However, it is also from this moment that he starts to disguise himself, at first with the bearing of a soldier (and probably with a vizard; see III.v.95 S.D.) and then, successively, as gaoler, tomb-maker, and the 'common bellman' sent to condemned criminals before their execution to remind them of heaven's mercy (see IV.i.80 and note; IV.ii.115, 172). He feels compelled to change his 'own shape' in order to show 'pity' and bring 'comfort' to the woman he has betrayed (see IV.i.133–8).

Webster's development of this character changes many other elements in the story. After being responsible for the Duchess's death, Bosola upbraids his master:

> *Bosola.* Fix your eye here.
> *Ferdinand.* Constantly.
> *Bosola.* Do you not weep?
>   Other sins only speak; murder shrieks out;
>   The element of water moistens the earth,
>   But blood flies upwards and bedews the heavens. (IV.ii.259–62)

When Ferdinand threatens him with death for what he has done and runs off 'much distracted', Bosola no longer has any doubt where his allegiance lies:

> What would I do, were this to do again?
> I would not change my peace of conscience
> For all the wealth of Europe. (IV.ii.338–40)

When the Duchess regains consciousness for a moment, after she had been left for dead, he sees a new hope. As the 'cords of life' break at last, the hired spy—now chief executioner as well—decides that 'somewhat I will speedily enact / Worth my dejection' (IV.ii.373–4). So ends the fourth Act, leaving the whole of the last in which, at risk of his own life, he tries to carry out that intention. He is the last of those who die in its 'great ruin' (V.v.111) and does so bravely, even though he knows he has no moral claim to courage:

> Let worthy minds ne'er stagger in distrust
> To suffer death or shame for what is just—
> Mine is another voyage. (V.v.103–5)

In some ways Webster is repeating the structure of *The White Devil*, which used Bracciano's secretary, Flamineo, as commentator on the life and death of his master and his own sister who is at first the Duke's mistress and then his wife. But Bosola is a tougher and less enthusiastic accomplice, and more involved on his own account with other persons in the play. Whereas at the very last moment Flamineo had learnt, 'Th'art a noble sister— / I love thee now' (V.vi.241–2), from Act III onwards Bosola is drawn, slowly and against his own choice, to admire and care for the Duchess. How far and in what sense he 'loves' her is not made clear in the text, but in performance the actor playing the role will always develop a very intimate contact with whoever is playing the Duchess, so closely involved are they with each other. Neither one can say his or her lines without being highly sensitive to the other, in tone, timing, pitch, feeling; both are required to maintain a mutual understanding through such deeply affecting events that they can scarcely avoid suggesting a hidden and delicate relationship between the two persons they represent.

Webster creates and handles his characters so that they reflect each other like mirrors, surprising the audience with what it sees and hears, changing perspective to encourage depths of understanding to which the characters of the play either have no access or from which they instinctively shy away from acknowledging. It is as if he has constructed a complicated intellectual structure and through its elaborations conducted and presented the play's comparatively simple but often sensational action.

The relationships of the central characters in *The Palace of Pleasure* are altered radically. The Cardinal becomes the younger, not the older, brother, and Ferdinand is made the twin of his sister, also younger but by no more than a few hours. With no warranty in the source, the Cardinal is provided with a mistress and, halfway through the play, takes off his priestly robes to become a soldier (III.iv). The younger twin becomes sexually aroused and painfully tormented in his sister's presence: he takes his father's poniard with him for a private encounter in the first Act, and threatens to use it; he brings it again to her bed-chamber in the third, leaving it there as if she should use it on herself. Yet Ferdinand never strikes with this dagger and, even when he is sure that her husband is listening (see III.ii.91), he does not force a confrontation with him. While Ferdinand intends to act boldly and decisively against his sister's marriage, he delays doing so until she is in prison and in the dark. In contrast, his brother, the Cardinal, does act against his sister as soon as the marriage is known: with notable 'violence' (III.iv.36), he takes off her wedding ring while she is making an act of devotion to Our Lady of Loretto (see III.iv.36–9). Ferdinand is so distracted by seeing the Duchess dead that he turns into a madman; and then he dies as if fighting in some heroic battle. In what is surely another purposeful contrast, the Cardinal becomes more secretive and devious during these concluding events, until he is confronted by Bosola and then he cries out in panic; as Bosola says, he falls faster of himself than 'calamity' can 'drive' him, as if his 'greatness was only outward' (V.v.42–4).

These reactions are very different from the behaviour of the Duchess when she meets adversity and the threat of madness—this last experience made actual for her by the presence of sexually explicit madmen—and Webster ensures that the audience is made aware of the contrasts by bringing the Duchess back to the stage after her death, both as an actual ghost and as the dominating force in the minds of others. Ferdinand seems to believe that she is the 'shadow' following him and treats all the people he sees around him as if they also were 'beasts for sacrifice', driven by appetite and by 'flattery and lechery' (V.ii.31–5, 79–81). Bosola, as he strives to raise the 'sword of justice', thinks that the Duchess 'haunts' him, and, following the precedent of Isabella in *The White Devil*, Webster might have intended her to reappear on stage at this point as an hallucination (see V.ii.344–6 and note). In Act V, scene iii, she is certainly present, speaking as an echo emanating from her own grave; and almost certainly, when Antonio says 'a clear light' shows him a 'face folded in sorrow' (ll. 44–5), an ingenious device makes her briefly visible again (see below, pp. 24–5). On his return to the stage, Ferdinand is still more obsessed with his sister, and with darkness and secrecy. 'Strangling is a very quiet death' (V.iv.34) are his first words, as if he were re-enacting her last moments in his maddened fantasy. In the concluding scene, immediately before his death, more coherent speech is driven by thoughts of her: she is 'the cause' of what has happened, and he knows that 'ambition, blood, or lust', or some potent mixture of them all, has left him hurtling towards inescapable disaster (V.v.71–3). As he warned in the very first scene, Ferdinand's darkest actions and most private thoughts have 'come to light' (I.i.315–16). Webster has altered his source so that two twins, Ferdinand and the Duchess, are both sexually aroused by a person that they fear to acknowledge to the world, and so that they suffer very differently for it.

In many ways, however, the Duchess stands alone at the centre of the play, its chief mystery and source of wonder. Unlike Ferdinand she does not question 'the cause' of her death, seeming to have no sense of the force of his motivation to kill her:

> Why might not I marry?
> I have not gone about, in this, to create
> Any new world, or custom. (III.ii.109–11)

Although entirely at the mercy of her executioners, she takes her own time in death, meeting it in her own chosen way:

> Pull, and pull strongly, for your able strength
> Must pull down heaven upon me.—
> Yet stay: heaven-gates are not so highly arched
> As princes' palaces; they that enter there
> Must go upon their knees.—[*Kneels.*] Come, violent death,
> Serve for mandragora to make me sleep!—
> Go tell my brothers, when I am laid out,
> They then may feed in quiet. *They strangle her.* (IV.ii.229–36)

Her very last words not only acquiesce in what has become inevitable, but also mock or taunt her persecutors (see note to text). Perhaps Webster's principal purpose is to display her fully and 'to the life', leaving the audience to question the cause, and the rights and wrongs, of her suffering.

Around this central female figure, Webster has set a crowd of males, ambitious courtiers, ready to vie with each other on horseback or in political business, or in laughter at the expense of themselves or of women. These help to define, and so to project, the nature of the Duchess, and, from among them, she makes 'choice' of husband, telling Antonio:

> If you will know where breathes a complete man—
> I speak it without flattery—turn your eyes
> And progress through yourself.   (I.i.435–7)

The slow love-scene between them is touched with self-deprecating and excited humour, shot through with fear, and encompasses both careful ritual and intimate physical contact. Sensual reality and psychological subtlety are here sustained for more than a hundred and forty lines, a feat unequalled among English plays surviving from this time. Perhaps the 'balcony scene' in *Romeo and Juliet* (II.i) comes closest, but there the two lovers are separated on different levels of the stage. *The Duchess of Malfi* is also rare among works contemporary with it in that its heroine takes the lead throughout the wooing; the delicacy with which this is handled is unique.

Around the Duchess, besides her brothers and the male courtiers, Webster has provided three women who also help to define, by contrast and reflection, the nature of her spirit. Cariola, the waiting-woman, is closest to her mistress and sensitive to both her strength and weakness. She is left alone at the end of the first Act to comment as the couple go to their marriage bed:

> Whether the spirit of greatness or of woman
> Reign most in her, I know not, but it shows
> A fearful madness. I owe her much of pity.   (I.i.504–6)

Despite misgivings, she stays with her mistress after 'wiser buntings' have gone (III.v.5–6); and in prison, as the Duchess is summoned to her death, she is there to cry out for help. Although intending to die with her mistress (see IV.ii.195–201), she is removed from the stage and killed later as she tries to save her own life by lies, and bites and scratches. At the beginning of Act II, an Old Lady is added to the

dramatis personae to act as midwife for the Duchess's first child, and
Webster also gives her an earlier entrance so that Bosola can casti-
gate her for face-painting and making a pretence to beauty and
youth. Bosola sends her off as a fit partner for old Castruchio, who
is the husband of Julia, the Cardinal's mistress. This third member
of the supporting cast of women is seen for the first time in Rome in
shocking intimacy with the prelate—another scene which has no
obvious equal for the physical contact its text requires. It will be no
surprise later when Julia prides herself on being one of the 'great
women of pleasure' (V.ii.192). The Cardinal's secrecy about their
relationship reflects obviously enough on that of the Duchess with
regard to Antonio, while Julia's unashamed sexuality contrasts with
Ferdinand's tortured expression of unfulfilled desire. In the last Act
she demands at pistol-point that Bosola should 'kill' her longing for
him and this, too, reflects upon the central figure of the drama. The
reasons Julia gives for wooing make those of the Duchess at the start
of the play seem, in retrospect, to be just as irrational, although not
so untroubled:

> Compare thy form and my eyes together,
> You'll find my love no such great miracle.
> Now you'll say
> I am wanton.—This nice modesty in ladies
> Is but a troublesome familiar
> That haunts them.   (V.ii.166–71)

When her attraction to Bosola proves the immediate cause of her
death, a further reflection of the Duchess is both close and challeng-
ingly different:

>   'Tis weakness
> Too much to think what should have been done.—I go,
> I know not whither.   (V.ii.286–8)

Webster's reflective, or analogical, dramatic structure is clearest of
all in a sequence of visual images he creates. At the start of both Act
I and Act II, the location is the presence chamber of the Duchess's
palace. On each occasion, the grouping around the central figure
will be much the same: everyone else, including her brothers, must
attend on the enthroned Duchess, standing with heads uncovered as
a mark of respect (see II.i.122–32); bowing or perhaps kneeling
before speaking, waiting in silence to catch her eye, watching rival

courtiers with suspicion. In the first scene, she has little to say, until the stage has cleared and she is alone with her brothers; in the second, she takes a more active part, but, being in the last stages of her first pregnancy, suddenly breaks all protocol, crying out in pain and having to be rushed from the scene. Act III starts without comparable formality but in one sense this is merely delayed. A short public scene shows 'the Lord Ferdinand . . . going to bed' (III.i.37–8) and then the location shifts to the Duchess's bed-chamber where, among jokes and game-playing, all is informal and Antonio is 'lord of mis-rule' (III.ii.7). Only after Ferdinand has surprised her, as she is brushing her tangled hair, do members of the court enter and suddenly the private space becomes public. The Duchess is once more the centre of attention, but without composure; in a dangerous situation, lies must be used to shield her honour, and 'short syllables / Must stand for periods' (III.ii.176–81).

The prison which is the setting of Act IV is a more formal presence chamber once again, although the visual resemblance to the first two Acts is not clear until the Madmen enter as in an anti-masque to entertain the Duchess with song-and-dance while their lecherous and obsessed talk threatens her composure. When Bosola ushers in her Executioners, with '*a coffin, cords, and a bell*', they are accompanied, as in a formal masque, with verses suitable for wedding or for funeral. He speaks explicitly of the similarity to the earlier ceremonial scenes, announcing that this is her 'last presence chamber' (IV.ii.165–70). Indeed, in this most continuously formal of all scenes, the Duchess cannot move from the central position: she is 'chained to endure' all that is presented to her (IV.ii.60). In the play's last Act, which takes place in Milan, the Duchess is no longer alive to be the 'presence' at centre stage; yet at the last moment, when Delio enters with the heir to her dukedom, everyone acknowledges the boy 'In 's mother's right' (V.v.113) with silent reverence similar to that which had accompanied her earliest appearance.

Webster's construction of visual stage-images which reflect one on each other is also evident in the dumb show which presents the Cardinal banishing the Duchess and her family from the shrine of Our Lady at Loretto. The very inclusion of this episode—it can be cut with no more damage to the play's narrative than rendering unnecessary a few lines in the previous scene—argues its importance to the author. A statue of the Virgin placed on stage sets the scene, so that two Pilgrims can comment:

First Pilgrim. I have not seen a goodlier shrine than this,
   Yet I have visited many.
Second Pilgrim. The Cardinal of Aragon
   Is this day to resign his cardinal's hat;
   His sister Duchess likewise is arrived
   To pay her vow of pilgrimage. I expect
   A noble ceremony.   (III.iv.1–7)

Instead of a line of people waiting to bow or kneel to her presence, the audience now sees how the Duchess and her family, having knelt and '*presented themselves at the shrine*', are banished from the state of Ancona by the Cardinal, newly invested with '*sword, helmet, shield, and spurs*' and forcing the wedding ring from his sister's finger. To achieve this demonstrative moment, Webster has modified his source, in which Pope Julius II was the prelate who became a soldier and the Cardinal obtained the banishment by applying diplomatic pressure not by his own direct intervention. The scene works visually in much the same layered way as a verbal pun: it is concerned with both power and humility, and it is simultaneously both religious and sacrilegious. While sight of a statue of the Virgin could provoke merciful and loving thoughts, the Cardinal proves to be military and unforgiving.

   The reflective nature of the scene becomes clearer after consulting the history of the Loretto shrine and the reputation of the Virgin throughout Christendom.[1] Prayers to the Mother of Christ were not established religious offices in Webster's England, nor was she widely reported, as in medieval times, to stand in the presence of God in heaven interceding for mercy on humankind's behalf. Her loving-kindness and devotion to her Son were, however, known to all who heard the Gospels read in English in parish churches throughout the land. Shakespeare in *All's Well that Ends Well* has the

---

1. A comparison with the scene of the Papal election in *The White Devil* (IV.iii) will show that in *The Duchess* Webster was developing a structural device he had used earlier (see Introduction, Revels Student Edition (1996), pp. 22–3). Both scenes have a startling visual centre, in which either nothing is said or only Latin is spoken. Both involve a visual transformation of a leading character and a protracted religious ceremony; both stage episodes that are incidental to their play's main action, holding back its forward narrative drive. While only in *The Duchess* does the heroine take part in the ceremony, in both plays later scenes which are crucial to the main story echo the formal stage-image so that the audience gains a fuller understanding of the central character and of the implications of what happens to her.

Countess hope for the Virgin's intercessions when she considers Bertram's actions:

> He cannot thrive,
> Unless her prayers, whom heaven delights to hear
> And loves to grant, reprieve him from the wrath
> Of greatest justice.   (III.iv.26–9)

The fame of the shrine at Loretto had spread across Europe. It was reputed to be Mary's very own home, having been transported miraculously from Galilee to Italy and now filled with treasures. It was dominated by a statue of the Virgin which was said to be a miraculously true likeness; princes would kneel there in reverence and leave rich gifts behind them.[2] If only a little of all this was common knowledge, a visual memory of the Loretto scene would have been awakened in the prison scene that shortly follows. When the Duchess stops her executioners so that she may kneel before death and become a petitioner in her own 'last presence chamber', she is repeating the ritual posture that she had taken before at the shrine of Our Lady. Later, when she returns to life—miraculously, it might seem—she calls Antonio's name and then speaks only the one word 'Mercy' (IV.ii.352), so naming the very gift for which the Virgin's prayers were said to plead. A little earlier, on her first stirring back to life, Bosola had had this same thought:

> Her eye opes,
> And heaven in it seems to ope, that late was shut,
> To take me up to mercy.   (IV.ii.346–8)

A distorted reflection of the Loretto scene and the Virgin's continuing concern for humankind may be heard, and perhaps seen, in Act V, when the Duchess, as an echo, speaks to Antonio by repeating the most appropriate and caring words from those that he and Delio have used. This scene is also in a holy place, and the echo's effect is almost miraculous, but it all takes place among ruins, not in a goodly shrine or at a noble ceremony. No statue of the Virgin is

---

2. For example, the Prince of Transylvania sent an image of Our Blessed Lady some two feet high and made of solid silver; it was 'of excellent workmanship and curiously inlaid with gold', and at its feet the donor was portrayed in full armour, as if praying (O. Torsellino, *History of Our B. Lady of Loretto*, tr. 1608, K3; the various miraculous circumstances and great wealth of the shrine are enumerated in this book).

seen here; that is now replaced by a brief and possibly imaginary view of the Duchess from within her grave and in her grave-clothes.

MEANINGS

Webster makes large demands upon his audience. The web of complex reflections which he creates as he tells his story invites careful attention, and in other respects his handling of action and dialogue goes beyond usual expectations. The presentation of Court life, with its scheming, pretences, and danger, raises questions about the simplest words and actions. Few of his characters can speak what they feel; they say only what they ought to say to satisfy those who control how they live their lives.

In some respects, Webster's treatment of the basic true-life story is almost incredible and tends towards absurdity. Julia as a wife for the old Castruchio, who is ambitious for success like the youngest courtier; childish quibbles in the letter Ferdinand sends to the banished Antonio; the notion of a pistol concealed in a codpiece— these are trivial examples. The Cardinal's being caught in his own safety precautions, so that his cries for help are thought to be game-playing, is an invention with more serious implications because it involves matters of life and death and touches upon the nature of one of the play's chief characters. Whereas Painter's *Palace of Pleasure* deals at length with the difficulties of keeping even one childbirth secret, Webster has two more children born to the Duchess between Acts II and III, and still the marriage is treated as secret while those who have learnt about it still have not recognized that Antonio is the husband; and at this point, Ferdinand, with opportunity to do so, does not discover this vital information. Some fateful actions happen by mere chance: Antonio dropping an astrological calculation concerning his child's nativity and Bosola killing Antonio:

> I know not how—
> Such a mistake as I have often seen
> In a play. (V.v.94–6)

Many readers will take these aspects of Webster's stagecraft as proof that he was an unskilful dramatist, but he might well have answered that charge as he did another in the preface to *The White Devil*, that 'willingly, and not ignorantly, in this kind have I faulted'. His stage techniques are appropriate for an author who saw that the world in which he lived could be, at times, strangely and even outrageously unbelievable, and also that individuals are only partly in charge of their fates.

The mental torture of the prison scene grips an audience's attention, and its slow development is progressively hard to bear, but, even here, where the drama is most narrowly compelling, the weirdness of Webster's invention will also tempt spectators to suspend belief in a way that is contrary to direct feeling. The dead man's hand and trick with lights, the waxwork models of father and children, the lewd madmen and their harsh, reiterative song, Bosola's successive disguises—all these allow no settled attitude to the relentless cruelty. When the Duchess asks that her 'little boy' should have 'Some syrup for his cold' and the girl 'Say her prayers, ere she sleep' (IV.ii.202–4), attention is pulled in yet another direction, towards pathetic sentiment. Nevertheless, here again, all this could be the result of the author's deliberate choice. Perhaps the very strange and (to use Webster's word) ingenious events are intended to make more remarkable the fact that the Duchess does not cry out in fear or 'panic', or moan or protest, or demand that justice be done, as her counterpart in Webster's source had done. 'I leave you to think what horror and trance assailed the feeble heart of this poor lady', wrote William Painter, and then proceeded to tell of her 'sighs and lamentations'. In sharp contrast, Webster's Duchess has a steadfast courage, and with clear insight views her position steadily, even when it is manifestly the product of her oppressor's deranged mind. In a wild, lunatic, and almost unbelievable world, forever shifting in its unpredictable cruelty, she becomes the one possible and stable centre for the audience's attention, evoking a response far less facile than horror and suffering alone could have solicited. A tendency to disbelieve what is happening can keep thrill and horror from overwhelming all other responses; only the Duchess's strength of mind and purpose holds unqualified attention and seems to grow in consequence.

Perhaps the audience is most tested, or remains most confused, by Webster's creation of certain characters whose 'faces do belie their hearts', who keep their actions and 'privat'st thoughts' to themselves (I.i.309–16) and may well remain unconscious of the inner forces which drive them. He provides no clear-cut verbal statement of Ferdinand's lust for his sister, or of Antonio's self-serving intentions, or of Bosola's inherent melancholy, as opposed to that 'garb of melancholy' which is merely a disguise. Similarly, the audience cannot be sure that Ferdinand is totally out of control in his madness or know why the Duchess does not dare to make her marriage public until it is too late.

From time to time, Webster gives his characters words which seem to reveal their private thoughts or sum up the nature of the world in which they live. These are easy to identify since they are often placed immediately before an exit or at the end of a scene or episode; following the first printing of the text, this edition prints many of them in italics. Such expressions of considered judgement were known as '*sententiae*' and were used by many writers of poetry and prose, as well as dramas. But too much reliance should not be placed on them. Webster collected such wise sayings from the very various books that he was reading while writing this play, so that they do not arise solely out of his understanding of the individual speakers in the developing drama. In *The White Devil*, Flamineo mocks the appearance of wisdom in 'a dried sentence, stuffed with sage' (IV.ii.247), and many in Webster's plays *are*, indeed, 'dried', or even dead when compared with lively interchange of dialogue or sustained soliloquy. They are like signposts, provided by the play's characters as they step out of character and out of dramatic time; or like stepping stones, on which an audience can keep some balance in the breathless rush and irregular eddies of the play's action.

More substantial and perhaps more durable in effect are two occasions when interchange of dialogue is halted for a story to be told. So, in his sister's bed-chamber just before he leaves, 'ta'en up in a whirlwind' to join his brother in Rome, Ferdinand takes time to begin a tale formally:

> Upon a time, Reputation, Love, and Death
> Would travel o'er the world; and it was concluded
> That they should part, and take three several ways ...   (III.ii.122ff.)

Similarly, when Bosola is about to lead the Duchess to prison, she stops him with:

> Sad tales befit my woe; I'll tell you one.
> A salmon, as she swam unto the sea,
> Met with a dogfish ...   (III.v.124ff.)

This story ends with a *sententia*: 'So, to great men, the moral may be stretched: / *Men oft are valued high when th'are most wretch'd*' (ll. 140–1). Bosola is given nothing to say in reply, and everyone is ready to leave the stage, but the Duchess delays them further. Accepting her powerlessness, she adds another *sententia* which is far more ambiguous in effect: '*There's no deep valley but near some great hill*' (l. 144). As the Act concludes, the audience cannot know whether she is resigned to death or hopes even yet for some reverse of fortune; her words can be interpreted both ways, and the telling of a story has ensured that the audience considers this.

The stories and *sententiae* provide meanings for moments, more or less credible and relevant. When Delio gives the final message of this sort, '*Integrity of life is fame's best friend, / Which nobly, beyond death, shall crown the end*' (V.v.120–1), the audience is offered words asserting that any possibility of satisfaction must be sought beyond the events of the play itself. Webster has not provided any one assured meaning for his tragedy but a succession of possible meanings, in sufficient number to keep his audience attentive and in sufficient variety to ensure that its members must choose between them. The play's argument is centred unmistakably on the Duchess, and her story provides an experience for the audience to live through during each performance, out of the reach of any description or summation which the dramatist could, or would, provide.

The whole play is written with quick sensitivity; its dialogue is flexible, vivid, nervous, and, at times, pressured. Only rarely does a speech build to a powerful statement that draws many issues together and gives a sense of completion. Rather, impetus gathers slowly and irregularly, and often it is lost quickly, as new ideas or feelings intervene. Many of the strongest passages are short, sharp, and perceptive, stopping further exchange and seeming to require a shift of attention before the drama can proceed. From the Duchess, such are: 'My laurel is all withered', 'I am Duchess of Malfi still' (III.v.93; IV.ii.141); from Ferdinand 'Her guilt treads on / Hot-burning coulters', 'Die then, quickly!', 'This darkness suits you well' (III.i.56–7; III.ii.71; IV.i.30); from Bosola, 'Look you, the stars shine still' (IV.i.100).

Sometimes a short and piercing speech, with its own sense of closure, yields a swift afterthought so that the speaker's mind seems to be driving speech ahead with renewed energy. In exchange of dialogue, passion can seem to overpower restraint, as in:

> *Ferdinand.* I have this night digged up a mandrake.
> *Cardinal.*   Say you?
> *Ferdinand.* And I am grown mad with 't.
> *Cardinal.*   What's the prodigy?
> *Ferdinand.* Read there—a sister damned! She's loose i'th' hilts,
>   Grown a notorious strumpet.
> *Cardinal.*   Speak lower.
> *Ferdinand.*   Lower?
>   Rogues do not whisper 't now, but seek to publish 't.   (II.v.1–5)

In a soliloquy or sustained speech, a speaker can appear at the mercy of his or her own thoughts and feelings, as they elude expression or are denied it. When wooing Antonio, the Duchess changes subject and mood repeatedly, as if she is uncertain and exposed to unwanted thoughts (see, for example, I.i.440–59, 490–503). When she sits brushing her hair, her mind seems to wander of its own volition, moving fitfully from present time to future, from fear to laughter, tenderness to reproof (see III.ii.58–71); her words seem to follow her thoughts rather than directing them.

Sometimes a huge leap from one idea to another shows that feelings have built up underneath what is said until they demand expression. Ferdinand struggles to control himself as he thinks of revenge on his sister and then, without any warning except a change of rhythm and tension, speaks of suicide and of a sin committed by himself, not by his sister:

>   So. I will only study to seem
> The thing I am not.—I could kill her now,
> In you, or in myself, for I do think
> It is some sin in us heaven doth revenge
> By her.   (II.v.62–6)

A reader of the text might miss the force of this, but when it is acted, with the change of intention and feeling that the text clearly demands, Ferdinand seems, in a moment almost, to turn from rage to a shuddering sense of guilt. Should the actor not recognize what is demanded, the Cardinal adds a comment that acts as a kind of stage direction—'Are you stark mad?'—after which Ferdinand immediately recovers his earlier intensity: 'I would have their bodies / Burnt in a coal-pit, with the ventage stopped' (ll. 66–7). Dialogue such as this requires both careful reading and a vivid imagination.

In some episodes, especially those in prose, the dialogue becomes heavily laden with descriptive detail, taking the hearers' minds outside the world of the play to that of the court or city in Webster's London. Bosola often has this kind of speech, especially at the beginning of the play where satire and mockery seem to be his normal mode of thought. But all characters operate in somewhat similar fashion. So Antonio speaks of atheists, bribes, fashion, magistrates, dancing, paralysis, prayers, looking-glasses (see I.i.155–205). He speaks to the Duchess of 'prattling' courtiers and she to him of tradesmen in the city who light their wares poorly so that their imperfections are not visible (I.i.423 and 431–4). The themes of the main story are brought into contact with the lives of the audience, in graphic instances, often driven home by a grotesque or garish humour; for example, Antonio speaks of marriage with reference to the 'weak delight' of seeing a little son 'ride a-cock-horse' or to a preacher's account of heaven and hell, as if it were a case of perpetual bliss or punishment; the Cardinal speaks of 'a tame elephant' being watched by a husband who has no idea how to manage the huge and exotic beast (I.i.393–5 and 400–3; II.iv.31–2).

Words, however, can stop altogether in favour of silence. Sometimes a particular action takes over, which can be inferred from the dialogue. Thus, Ferdinand shows his father's poniard, the Duchess puts her ring to Antonio's eye, and they kneel together; so she eats apricots and waits for madmen to enter; and kneels again before death. Yet Webster uses silence more frequently than these actions indicate, using incomplete verse-lines to mark where a pause is required. The effect is that of a stalling aircraft, the forward drive of the story being halted and attention drawn to an impasse caused by the inner force of thought or feeling. On one occasion, Webster places a group of characters to comment on the 'deformed silence' of others: they see an 'eager violence' betrayed in Ferdinand's eye and an ominous lifting of the Cardinal's head; they sense the 'pangs' of life and death (III.iii.48–75).

The style of *The Duchess* is very like that of *The White Devil*, but used with a greater economy which gives a stronger forward drive and also, at times, a greater precision. Sometimes this new simplicity has a gentleness which was missing from the earlier play and renders the speaker more fully or more hopelessly exposed. So the Duchess confesses artlessly to Bosola: 'This good one that you speak of is my husband' (III.ii.278); and so Ferdinand says almost as affectingly, 'Let me see her face again' before turning in anger to accuse Bosola of lack of feeling (IV.ii.271). Occasionally the note is sustained, as by Ferdinand, speaking of love that might be found amongst 'unambitious shepherds' and 'quiet kindred' (III.ii.127–30) or by the Duchess, sustaining the note at greater length and with a more resilient rhythm:

> The birds that live i'th' field
> On the wild benefit of nature live
> Happier than we; for they may choose their mates,
> And carol their sweet pleasures to the spring.   (III.v.18–21)

In his madness, Ferdinand occasionally sounds the same note in the midst of his agony, though very briefly: 'I have cruel sore eyes', 'Strangling is a very quiet death', and 'The pain's nothing' (V.ii.64; V.iv.34; V.v.59).

Because Webster's writing has the power to represent unspoken thought, as well as intentional and instinctive speech, and to surprise continually by its shifts and silences, the play seems to 'live' in performance throughout its varied and often sensational action. This indicates the kind of attention it requires from a reader: a response to an illusion of lived experience, rather than a careful elucidation of the words of text alone. It also implies that the tragedy, for all its careful references to the court and city and for all its elaborate structure and eye-catching events, is grounded in its characters and the complexity and subtlety of their inner lives. Their very existence in on-stage reality is what most challenges an audience's accepted notions of female and male, power and dependence, success and failure, nobility and virtue, responsibility and independence, knowledge of the world and self-knowledge, pleasure and innocence, and all the many other issues raised in the play. The characters are the play's greatest strength and source of provocation.

EARLY PERFORMANCES

The stage-life of *The Duchess of Malfi* has been more continuous and better documented than that of most plays of its time, with the obvious exception of Shakespeare's. It was the first play in English to be printed with a cast-list of the actors for individual parts. (It is reproduced here, in its original form, before the *Dramatis Personae*.) The naming of two actors for each of three major roles enables the first performance to be dated no later than the death of William Ostler, the first Antonio, on 16 December 1614; one or more revivals followed some time after 1619 when Richard Burbage, the first Ferdinand, died and when Henry Condell, the first Cardinal, seems

to have turned from acting to management. These later performances were probably close in date to the play's publication in 1623,
since John Thompson, who is the only actor assigned to Julia, is
known for a series of female roles in plays by John Fletcher which
date from 1621, and Robert Pallant, who played both Cariola and
the doctor, would have been only sixteen in 1621 and so only just
experienced enough to play the doctor's scene (V.ii.1–84) opposite
a powerful Ferdinand. John Rice had been a boy in the company in
1610; he left soon after to rejoin in 1619, still very young to play the
'noble old fellow' Pescara.

Only one actor, Richard Sharp, is assigned to the Duchess, and
this also must refer to a revival, since his other known female roles
all date from 1616 onwards. The three principals for the first performances were all mature and highly experienced actors. John
Lowin, the Bosola, was in his late thirties. His quality is suggested by
his other roles, which included Shakespeare's Falstaff and Henry
VIII, Jonson's Morose, Volpone, and Mammon. The character of
Bosola was considered so important that the part was placed, against
all precedent, at the head of the Actors' List, instead of being
relegated to a position appropriate to his social standing. Richard
Burbage, the first Ferdinand, was the foremost actor of his time
and was then in his mid-forties. He was famous for roles as demand-
ing and varied as Shakespeare's Richard III, Othello, Hamlet, and
Lear. An elegy of 1619 praises his ability to give 'just weight' to his
delivery and also his 'enchanting tongue'; he could act 'a sad lover,
with so true an eye / That there I would have sworn, he meant
to die'.

Less is known of Henry Condell, but he was of the same genera-
tion as Burbage, and together they must have proved very strong
opposites for the boy actor playing the Duchess, Ferdinand's twin
sister. She is a 'lusty widow' (I.i.340) or, as she says, a 'young widow'
(I.i.460); the Cardinal is the younger of the two brothers. Perhaps
the differences in age and experience worked to the play's advantage
by accentuating an innocence in the Duchess and giving credibility
to Ferdinand's cry, 'she died young' (IV.ii.263), as if she remains
untouched by the years of the play's narrative and the tortures she
has endured. She dominated the experience given by the play: two of
the commendatory verses remember it by how the Duchess had
spoken or had been 'lively bodied' in performance; one of these
specifies the experience of *seeing* her 'live and die'. Some satirical
verses of 1632 speak, incidentally, of 'the Malfi duchess' being

conveyed 'sadly on her way', followed by many coaches for the mourners.

The title-page of 1623 claims that the tragedy had been 'presented privately at the Blackfriars, and publicly at the Globe', and that the published text included 'diverse things printed, that the length of the play would not bear in the presentment'. Nothing indicates which parts had been cut, but modern productions have shown that cohesion does not suffer from numerous small cuts in almost every scene. The fits and starts of some speeches and the occasional accumulation of descriptive details accommodate such changes with comparative ease, however unfortunate any particular loss may be. Larger cuts can be made at the beginning of Act I and II: the Officer's comments and Bosola's praise of Antonio in III.ii; the military talk before Bosola's arrival in III.iii; the Madmen's manic chatter; Antonio, Delio, and Julia's negotiations with Pescara in V.i. Nineteenth-century revivals cut Julia altogether from the play: it is fairly easily done. Removal of the Loretto and Echo scenes (III.iv and V.iii) also leaves no gap in the play's narrative line and so one or both of them are often dropped. However, Webster would surely have valued the change of pace and focus which they bring, and their spectacle and thematic significance. Besides, both have a major effect on the presentation of the Duchess without making particularly large demands on the young male actor. For all these reasons, they should probably be held sacrosanct.

The Echo scene includes one of three stage effects which suggest that the play was written especially for performance at the Blackfriars, and would not have been so effective at the Globe. In itself an Echo was not particularly rare in plays of the time, but a stage direction at the head of the scene—'*Echo from the Duchess' grave*'—indicates that more is required here than a voice coming mysteriously from somewhere off-stage. Yet more unusual is that Antonio thinks the speaker becomes visible within her grave: 'and on the sudden, a clear light / Presented me a face folded in sorrow' (V.iii.44–5). It so happened that the King's Men owned a piece of stage machinery that could do just that: it was described very specifically in a stage direction for *The Second Maiden's Tragedy*: '*On a sudden in a kind of noise like a wind, the doors clattering, the tombstone flies open, and a great light appears in the midst of the tomb; his Lady, as [she] went out, standing just before him all in white*'. The King's Men performed this play in 1611, within a year or so of taking over the indoors Blackfriars where a darkened stage could make good use of such an effect. Perhaps Webster had seen this ingenious stage-property lying unused and recycled it to his own advantage.

Light effects were specially apt for the Blackfriars, as shown by stage directions in Ben Jonson's *Catiline*, staged by the King's Men around 1611: '*A darkness comes over the place*', and six lines later, '*A fiery light appears*' (I.i.312–20). The darkness called for by Ferdinand in Act IV, scene i, would be most effective if it were an actual darkness, especially when he offers his sister a dead man's severed hand, which she takes as if she were greeting a living husband.

Webster's arrangement of the action into five acts is the third feature which suggests a play written especially for the Blackfriars. Whereas *The White Devil* had a continuous movement forward, with only one major time-gap between Acts IV and V, *The Duchess* requires considerable passages of time between each act, including one of several years between II and III. Little or no preparation is provided for these forward jumps, and only the briefest explanation afterwards, so that the play works best when the act divisions are clearly marked. This would always have been the case at the Blackfriars, where a group of musicians was maintained to play between the acts. Much of their music was written by Robert Johnson, who is cited as composer in one of the manuscripts of the Madman's song in *The Duchess*. Act intervals would have added to performance time and necessitated cuts, but on the other hand the greater intimacy of this indoors theatre would have been well suited to the silences and quiet passages which are also new features of this text.

After *The Duchess*, Webster probably wrote a play, which is now lost, called *The Guise*. He mentioned this in a Preface to *The Devil's Law Case* (1623), his tragicomedy about citizens, lawyers, and young noblemen which had had its first performance around the year 1617. A Lord Mayor's Pageant also followed, commissioned by the Merchant Taylors' Company to which Webster himself belonged as one of a family of coachbuilders, and also several plays written in collaboration with Ford, Rowley, Dekker, Middleton, Massinger, and Heywood. None of these was to make such a mark as *The Duchess*, which must have been revived at least once more after its publication so that it was available for performance before the King on 26 December 1630, in the new Cockpit Theatre at Whitehall. Webster died at about this time, or some time in the next decade. No writings have survived from after the late 1620s, and he was not commissioned to write the pageant when another Merchant Taylor was chosen as Lord Mayor of London in 1630.

A second edition of *The Duchess* appeared in 1640, an indication perhaps of further revivals.

After the banning of plays during the civil war, there are records of performances in 1662, 1668, and, at Court, in 1686. A Quarto edition of 1678 advertised itself with 'As it is now acted at the Duke's Theatre'; Thomas Betterton, leading actor of the company, is named as the Bosola and Mrs Betterton as the Duchess. In his *Roscius Anglicanus* (1708), John Downes assessed its record as 'exceedingly excellently acted in all parts, chiefly Duke Ferdinand and Bosola; it filled the House eight days successively, it proving one of the best of stock tragedies'. Another Quarto dated 1708 accompanied a revival in that year; it had a new title, *The Unfortunate Duchess of Malfi, or the Unnatural Brothers: a tragedy*, and shows which cuts were made in the text, including the Loretto scene (III.iv), the reputation and salmon stories, and the lines referring to the son of the first marriage (III.iii.69–71). Changes were made to regularize metre and modernize vocabulary, and to make the play more respectable (for example, 'lecher' became 'lover' at III.ii.100 and 'I pour it in your bosom' was omitted at III.i.52). More stage directions were added.

In 1735, Lewis Theobald published a radical reworking, entitled *The Fatal Secret*. On a par with Nahum Tate's rewriting of *King Lear*, this version reunites the Duchess and Antonio at the end of the play, together with a twelve-year-old son; the scene is Malfi throughout and the action starts after the marriage; Julia is omitted. The nineteenth century saw another version by R. H. Horne: the Duchess is now called Marina and her death is off-stage; and again there is no Julia. This text became popular as a star-vehicle for actresses: Miss Isabella Glyn at Sadler's Wells in 1850 and for many subsequent tours, and then in a new production, under her 'immediate Direction', at the Standard, Shoreditch in 1868; and Mrs Emma Waller at the Broadway, New York, in 1858 and for several subsequent tours. The *Lady's Newspaper* (23 November 1850) called Miss Glyn's Duchess:

> one of the most striking achievements of that rising actress. The scenes, intrinsically coarse, in which she makes love to her steward, were admira-

bly softened by the playful spirit of coquetry which she infused into them. The soft passages of sorrow stole with mournful effect upon the naturally mirthful temperament, and, when her wrongs aroused her alike to a sense of pain and dignity, her denunciations were terrific.

A Bosola by George Bennett at Sadler's Wells was the only other performance to attract much interest in the nineteenth century. Westland Marston's *Our Recent Actors*, ii (1888) recalls that in the prison scene (IV.ii): 'there was something in his servile appearance, in his deep, sepulchral tones, slow movements, and watchful, deliberate revelation of the coming horror, that seemed as if he himself had had such near commerce with Death as to be the fit representative of his terrors to the living' (p. 61). In 1892, for two performances only, the Independent Theatre Society produced *The Duchess*. It was one of the earliest of a series of English Renaissance plays directed by William Poel in what he considered to be an authentic manner. Henry Irving, however, lent costumes and scenery from his pictorial productions at the Lyceum and the text was altered by Poel so that Julia was excised and a 'Dance of Death' added.

In the twentieth century, Poel's initiative was followed and fuller texts used. The earliest, again for two performances only, was by the Phoenix Society at the Lyric, Hammersmith, with Cathleen Nesbitt as the Duchess and Edith Evans as Julia, who was now restored to the play; the director was Allan Wade. The year 1935 saw a production at the small Embassy Theatre, Swiss Cottage, and 1937 another at the Gate in Dublin. The play's arrival in the West End of London had to wait until 1945 in a production at the Haymarket by the scholar-director George Rylands: Peggy Ashcroft was the Duchess, John Gielgud, Ferdinand, and Cecil Trouncer, Bosola. Rylands again directed the play the following year at the Ethel Barrymore in New York, in a version by the poet W. H. Auden and with music by Benjamin Britten; Elisabeth Bergner was the Duchess and David Eccles Ferdinand, with the Afro-American Canada Lee playing Bosola in white-face. In all these productions in the first half of the twentieth century, the Duchess herself took most attention, but Gielgud's Ferdinand made such a lasting impression that, in 1960, Kenneth Tynan still remembered the 'thrill of finality' he gave to 'I will never see thee more' while Harold Hobson found that his 'torment of spirit . . . still excites the imagination' (*Observer* and *Sunday Times*, London, 18 December 1960). Cecil Trouncer, at the Haymarket in 1945, was the most successful of the Bosolas; his 'vital study, of . . . a murderer of fortune prematurely aged in the galleys', according to *The Times* (London), was the 'supreme attraction of the revival'.

As a whole, the play was less enthusiastically welcomed. Unwanted laughter or an absence of necessary horror were variously noted by the critics. Webster's handling of emotion was branded 'mediocre' (see, for example, p. 1, above), his characterization muddled or incomprehensible, the plotting clumsy and crude, the horrors cheaply sensational. In particular the fifth Act was considered irredeemable. Later productions did little, at first, to vindicate the play's dramatic structure or Webster's theatrical skill. After a 1957 revival at the Phoenix, New York, directed by Jack Landau with Jacqueline Brookes as the Duchess, *Theatre Arts* found the play was 'curiously episodic, and the episodes are somehow not cumulative'. After a production in 1960 by the Royal Shakespeare Company at the Aldwych Theatre, London, with Peggy Ashcroft again playing the Duchess, Harold Hobson said that the play had 'no drive, no force, no continuity', as if the director had decided that 'it is in single lines that the genius of Webster lies'. Another RSC production in 1971 starred Judi Dench as the Duchess and again, for the critics, this character and her finer feelings dominated the evening. At the Manchester Royal Exchange in 1981, Helen Mirren was a Duchess who drew strength from her sexual nature and instinctive intelligence. At the National Theatre in London in 1985 the play had a more general effect, although its cast included Ian McKellan as a sharp-minded Bosola and Eleanor Bron as a splendid and sensitive Duchess. In this instance critics found the production underpowered and blamed the director, Philip Prowse, for giving too much scope to his own taste for sumptuous and macabre settings designed by himself.

Despite all this negative publicity, the play is now staged with greater frequency. Small-scale companies which can draw on good actors fare the best and can do most to vindicate both Webster's dramatic structure and his vision of the world. An example was Peter Gill's 1971 production for the Royal Court Theatre in London. Set starkly on the small stage without scenery and only the simplest furniture, it looked reminiscent of the lunatic asylum in Peter Brook's world-famous production of *Marat/Sade* (1964). Instead of a fully fledged and splendid Court, a chorus of actors, uniformly and drabbly dressed, remained on stage throughout the play to act as scenery as well as the many smaller characters. This treatment exposed some inadequate casting, but the Duchess of Judy Parfitt was seen not only for her virtues but also in a deep-seated, unavoidable, and pervasive predicament. In 1995, a production by Philp Franks, an actor turned director, started at the Greenwich Theatre on the outskirts of London and then, after a tour which was, in effect, an extended rehearsal, reached London at Wyndham's Theatre. Juliet Stevenson, as the Duchess, took time in her scenes with Antonio to realize the sexual interplay and subtlety of thought with a realism closer to film than theatre. This slowed down the play's action but helped Simon Russell Beale's Ferdinand to make a claim for equal attention, using similarly explicit means to express his sexual desire for his sister, but in a crude and infantile manner. This double focus, in an intimate theatre, together with a spare visual presentation, allowed Webster's narrative to grip the audience so that the usual chorus of critical disapproval of his theatrical judgement was almost silenced.

The reinstatement of the dramatist as a master of theatre was continued by Cheek by Jowl, a company whose work has often been as adventurous and bare-faced as its name. Their production toured extensively in 1995 and followed the one from Greenwich into the same London theatre early in 1996. This *Duchess of Malfi* was unusual for the freedom with which the actors had been encouraged to find their own ways with their characters, tuning and turning the text to suit their own temperaments and abilities. Anastasia Hille played the Duchess with an imperious and often cynical intelligence; she was restless, aggressive, dismissive, laughed harshly or nervously, and then suddenly spoke the most affecting lines with a surprising simpleness. Scott Handy's Ferdinand was a badly behaved boy-man, given to fights and hugs with his sister. A small but physically varied group of actors were successively courtiers, officers, priests, soldiers, torturers, and doctors (for the Lycanthropic episode in V.ii.1–83). By their means the director was able to keep the audience alert to the context of the main action. They were used with eye-catching invention but, in the more formal scenes, they stood around like dummies. At the end of the play, the director gave a greater sense of cohesion than the text suggests by having all the principals rise from death to pose as if for a family photograph. The strong individualism evident in this production, both in its acting and direction, regained for the play an approbation which has not been so evident since its early stage history.

PUBLICATION

The Quarto edition of 1623 was marked as authoritative by generous prefatory material and its title-page, complete with a Latin motto ascribed to Horace (in its abbreviated form meaning something like 'If you know better kindly tell us; if not use this with me'). It was thicker than most plays, only three printed between 1615 and 1645 coming within a dozen of its 104 pages. Its text was clearly divided into acts and scenes (marked in Latin) and all the persons entering a scene were named together at its head in the manner approved for classical and neo-classical plays. A stage direction, *'The author disclaims this ditty to be his'* (opposite III.iv.8–11), shows clearly that the author was involved in this publication—something that could not be taken for granted at this time.

Bibliographical research has now provided more information. First, the 'true and exact copy' mentioned on the title-page was *not* the author's manuscript as might be expected, but a copy of the play made by a professional scribe, who was almost certainly Ralph Crane, who worked for the King's Men from before 1621. Second, variants among different copies of the Quarto show that the press was frequently stopped to make corrections as printing was in progress. This process was not very thorough, because obvious errors remain, but some of the new readings are not corrections of misreadings which could have been derived from consulting the printer's copy—including the addition of the note about the 'ditty' (which in the uncorrected form of another stage direction was called a 'Hymn'). These particular corrections and at least six added stage directions show that Webster actually visited the press and took an interest in the text's authenticity.

Insufficient evidence survives to show for certain the kind of manuscript from which Crane worked, but the absence of a prompter's additions or other characteristics of a copy made for use in a theatre, together with the general clarity of the text, argue that it was close to the author's own manuscript. Some 'authorial' loose ends support this hypothesis: for example, the 'ghost' character of Forobosco, who is named in the text but not in any stage direction, and the confusion about the identity of the various Madmen in IV.ii.

Nicholas Oakes, the printer, had only one press in 1623 and limited quantities of type, so that the two compositors who set the text worked simultaneously on alternate groups of four pages. They also set all pages on one side of the sheet of paper out of which four quarto leaves would be folded and cut, and then those on the other side. This maximized the use of type and meant that, in any 'gathering' of eight consecutive pages, 2, 3, 6, and 7 would be set first, and then 1, 4, 5, and 8. To work in this way, the manuscript copy had to be 'cast off' to show what lines went on which pages. For this book these calculations were not always correct and therefore, on some pages, the compositor had to alter the verse-lining in his copy so that the text took up more space; on others he had to compress his material, sometimes setting verse as if it were prose. Stage directions were sometimes moved so that they could be fitted in where space was available.

The printed text moved further away from Webster's manuscript because Crane followed his own preferences in punctuation, spelling, lining, use of capitals, and forms of abbreviation and elision. Almost certainly, he removed many stage directions he found in his copy as if he, or someone acting as editor, trusted the words of the text to say all that was necessary. The compositors, too, had licence to introduce changes in the 'accidentals' of their copy, so that they would alter spelling and punctuation to please themselves and to utilize the type as best they could to keep the presses printing.

Either the author, scribe, or editor made sure that the text as published did not contain profanities. *The White Devil* has seven oaths using God's name, while *The Duchess* has none. Nor does anyone speak of God in the later play, whereas in the earlier this happens on sixteen occasions. Censorship has been at work, but that does not entirely account for these differences between the two plays. While *The Duchess* refers to 'heaven' or 'the heavens' as many as thirty times, compared with the *Devil*'s eleven, on fourteen occasions 'heaven' or 'the heavens' could not have replaced an earlier 'God', because that would not have fitted either the sense or the metre. Clearly the author's interest while writing the later play had shifted from the idea of a personal God to a concern with the impersonal 'heavens o'er our heads'. The three or four occasions when an original 'God' may have been censored out are discussed in annotations to the present edition.

THIS EDITION

The text printed here is that of the first Quarto of 1623 (referred to as Q), incorporating all press corrections that have been found. Where appropriate, entries have been moved from the beginning of scenes to where they should occur in the text. When these have been emended or had material added, and also when new stage directions have been supplied to clarify the stage action, all editorial changes are printed within square brackets.

Q marks some of the *sententiae* with italic type, insetting, or quotation marks; all these passages have been printed here in italics. Spelling and the use of capitals and italics have been modernized throughout. The same procedure has been used for elisions and contractions, except in those instances where metre, stress, or sense would have been affected.

Webster's style of writing for the stage means that punctuation cannot always be modernized according to standard rules. More than the usual numbers of colons and semi-colons are needed to show connections between units of speech or thought which would otherwise be marked as separate sentences by the use of full stops. Occasionally dashes are needed to show a rapid shift of attention or purpose which could not be signalled otherwise. In punctuating this text, a modern editor has many other issues to bear in mind besides ease of reading: Crane's interference with his copy, the compositors' preferences, temporary type-shortages, and whatever can be gathered of Webster's preferences from a study of the *White Devil* Quarto of 1612, which was set from an authorial manuscript.

The verse-lining of the Quarto has been corrected where it is plainly wrong. However what is required is not always obvious, nor what is prose rather than verse. Here this edition favours the least prescriptive form, sometimes printing what might possibly be very irregular verse as prose, and printing some verse in incomplete lines, rather than drawing two half-lines together as one. Such arrangements are occasional features of the *White Devil* Quarto.

Where necessary the Quarto text has been emended. Most of these changes are corrections of obvious mistakes or misreadings; some clarify unnecessary obscurities or irregularities, while others make a choice been two possible modern forms. However, some emendations, and some additions to the stage directions, do affect sense or the action on stage in significant ways and these are discussed, and alternative readings considered, in the annotations to the text.

FURTHER READING

The Revels Plays edition of 1964, by the present editor, still provides the fullest account of the first publication of *The Duchess* and of its textual authority and history. This is also the most convenient place to find a reprint of Webster's source for the play, William Painter's *Palace of Pleasure*; the text of the first edition of 1567 is reprinted, supplied with references to verbal echoes in the play. A list of readings from the second edition of 1575, which was 'corrected and augmented' by Painter, shows where Webster also borrowed from this version.

Two books can take a student further into the literary background of the play: Gunnar Boklund's '*The Duchess of Malfi*', *Sources, Themes, Characters* (Cambridge, Mass.: Harvard University Press, 1962) and R. W. Dent, *John Webster's Borrowing* (Berkeley and Los Angeles: University of California Press, 1960). The latter documents the books from which Webster took many *sententiae* and elaborate verbal images to work into his dialogue; the original versions are quoted in full, so that they may be compared with the rehandling of them, thus providing the means for a close-up, minuscule view of the workings of the dramatist's mind. Much of Dent's material can also be found in the Revels Plays annotations. The ample, learned, and often curious notes of F. L. Lucas's pioneering edition of Webster's *Works* in four volumes (London: Chatto & Windus, 1927) are also worth consulting in this connection: they give a panoramic view of the mental milieu in which Webster worked and from which he drew inspiration. Convenient and well-documented access to the social and political milieu of the times can be found in G. P. V. Akrigg's *Jacobean Pageant* (London: Hamish Hamilton, 1962).

All that is known or can be conjectured responsibly about Webster's life and career is to be found in two books published in the 1980s. The first was M. C. Bradbrook's *John Webster: Citizen and Dramatist* (London: Weidenfeld & Nicolson, 1980), and this was followed in 1986 by Charles R. Forker's *Skull Beneath the Skin: The Achievement of John Webster* (Carbondale and Edwardsville: Southern Illinois University Press). The latter volume, containing a comprehensive account of the work of earlier scholars and critics, provides a convenient starting point for anyone wishing to follow in these footsteps.

Several anthologies provide selections of earlier writings about the play. Don D. Moore's *John Webster and His Critics, 1617–1964* (Baton Rouge: Louisiana State University Press, 1966) is the most useful for early opinions and criticism, but necessarily the fuller tide of academic publishing that occured after the 1950s is barely represented. For that, a student should turn to the *Twentieth Century Interpretations of 'The Duchess of Malfi'*, ed. Norman Rabkin

(Englewood Cliffs, N.J.: Prentice-Hall, 1968); *John Webster*, edited by G. K. and S. K. Hunter in the Penguin Critical Anthologies series (Harmondsworth: Penguin, 1969); *Webster: 'The White Devil' and 'The Duchess of Malfi': A Casebook*, edited by R. V. Holdsworth (London: Macmillan, 1975); and *John Webster's 'The Duchess of Malfi'* in the Modern Critical Interpretations series, edited by Harold Bloom (New York, etc.: Chelsea House Publishers, 1987). The last named has the advantages of much the latest date and a concentration on the single play. Brian Morris's *John Webster* in the Mermaid Critical Commentary series (London: Ernest Benn, 1970) is an anthology of previously unpublished studies and consequently more unequal and of rather more specialist interest.

Study of *The Duchess* has usually gone hand-in-hand with a study of Webster's earlier *White Devil* which has so much in common in structure, characterization, spectacle, style, and theme that it may be considered a twin tragedy, the two works conceived at almost the same time and intended to complement each other. Most of the recommended reading about *The Duchess* is to be found in books dealing with both plays equally. At the head of the list is Travis Bogard's *The Tragic Satire of John Webster* (Berkeley and Los Angeles: University of California Press, 1955), a thoughtful attempt to account for Webster's unique mixture of dramatic modes. This line of enquiry was also taken by Jacqueline Pearson's commentary on the plays in *Tragedy and Tragicomedy in the Plays of John Webster* (Manchester: Manchester University Press, 1980) and Ralph Berry's *The Art of John Webster* (Oxford: Clarendon Press, 1972).

From the 1980s onwards, critics have tended to pursue one of three areas of study. First, the two heroines have been reappraised in the light of women's place in the society of the time and of other plays which present independent, unruly, or dissident heroines. Necessarily the scope of these books is normally far wider than Webster's two tragedies, as exemplified by Lisa Jardine's *Still Harping on Daughters: Women and Drama in the Age of Shakespeare* (Totowa, N.J.: Barnes & Noble, 1983). Joyce E. Peterson's *Curs'd Example: 'The Duchess of Malfi' and Commonweal Tragedy* (Columbia and London: University of Missouri Press, 1978) had its origin in an attempt to understand what the Duchess means when she says 'I am Duchess of Malfi still': the result is less a feminist interpretation than a sifting of textual evidence about character in moralistic terms. The second area of study has dealt with the wider social, political, and intellectual background of the play. One of the first, and still useful for its keen-eyed enquiry and wide scope, was Walter Lever's *The Tragedy of State* (London: Methuen, 1971); the chapter concerning Webster is reprinted in the *Casebook* anthology cited above. A later study, with particular focus on legal practice and the realities of political power, is Dena Goldberg, *Between Worlds: A Study of the Plays of John Webster* (Waterloo, Ontario: Wilfrid Laurier University Press, 1987).

The stage history of the play has become a third field of study, first marked by Richard Cave's '*The White Devil*' and '*The Duchess of Malfi*' in the Text and Performance series (London: Macmillan, 1988). This provides first-hand and critical accounts of productions at the Royal Court Theatre, London, in 1971 and the National Theatre in 1985. The achievements of the two *The Duchess of Malfi*s seen in the West End of London during the 1995/6 season are assessed by the present editor in *Shakespearean Illuminations: Insights from Performance*, ed. Jay L. Halio and Hugh Richmond (Newark: University of Delaware Press, 1997).

THE DUCHESS
OF MALFI

[DEDICATION]

To the Right Honourable George Harding, Baron Berkeley of
Berkeley Castle, and Knight of the Order of the Bath to the
Illustrious Prince Charles.

My Noble Lord,

That I may present my excuse why, being a stranger to your   5
Lordship, I offer this poem to your patronage, I plead this
warrant: men who never saw the sea, yet desire to behold that
regiment of waters, choose some eminent river to guide them
thither, and make that, as it were, their conduct or postilion;
by the like ingenious means has your fame arrived at my   10
knowledge, receiving it from some of worth who both in
contemplation and practice owe to your Honour their clearest
service. I do not altogether look up at your title, the ancientest
nobility being but a relic of time past, and the truest honour
indeed being for a man to confer honour on himself, which   15
your learning strives to propagate and shall make you arrive at
the dignity of a great example. I am confident this work is not
unworthy your Honour's perusal; for by such poems as this,
poets have kissed the hands of great princes and drawn their
gentle eyes to look down upon their sheets of paper when the   20
poets themselves were bound up in their winding sheets. The
like courtesy from your Lordship shall make you live in your
grave and laurel spring out of it, when the ignorant scorners of

---

1. *George Harding*] Son of Sir Thomas Berkeley by Elizabeth Carey
(daughter of George, Lord Hunsdon), he was born 7 October 1601. In 1619
he became a student at Christ Church College, Oxford. He travelled widely
and died in 1658. While still at university he received the dedication of
Robert Burton's *Anatomy of Melancholy* (1621), and later, in 1630, gave the
author the church living of Seagrave, Leicestershire. Some years after
Webster's dedication, he received those of Massinger's *Renegado* (1621) and
Shirley's *Young Admiral* (1637).

9. *conduct*] conductor, escort.
postilion] guide, forerunner.

11–13. *some . . . service*] perhaps the King's Men, who as the Chamber-
lain's Men had 'served' Lord Hunsdon (see l. 1, note above); *clearest* =
unqualified, most entire.

13. *look up at*] feel respect for.

the Muses (that like worms in libraries seem to live only to
destroy learning) shall wither, neglected and forgotten. This   25
work and myself I humbly present to your approved censure,
it being the utmost of my wishes to have your honourable self
my weighty and perspicuous comment; which grace so done
me, shall ever be acknowledged

By your lordship's   30
in all duty and observance,
John Webster.

[COMMENDATORY VERSES]

In the just worth of that well-deserver, Mr. John Webster, and upon
this masterpiece of tragedy.

In this thou imitat'st one rich and wise,
That sees his good deeds done before he dies;
As he by works, thou by this work of fame   5
Hast well provided for thy living name.
To trust to others' honourings is worth's crime;
Thy monument is raised in thy lifetime.
And 'tis most just; for every worthy man
Is his own marble, and his merit can   10
Cut him to any figure and express
More art than Death's cathedral palaces,
Where royal ashes keep their court. Thy note
Be ever plainness, 'tis the richest coat;
Thy epitaph, only the title be—   15
Write, 'Duchess', that will fetch a tear for thee,
For whoe'er saw this duchess live and die,
That could get off under a bleeding eye?

---

26. *approved censure*] tested judgement.
28. *perspicuous*] perhaps 'discerning' rather than, more properly, 'lucid'.

In Tragaediam.

Ut lux ex tenebris ictu percussa tonantis,   20
Illa, ruina malis, claris sit vita poetis.
                    Thomas Middletonus,
                        Poeta & Chron. Londinensis.

To his friend, Mr. John Webster, upon his *Duchess of Malfi.*

I never saw thy duchess till the day   25
That she was lively bodied in thy play;
Howe'er she answered her low-rated love,
Her brothers' anger did so fatal prove,
Yet my opinion is, she might speak more,
But never, in her life, so well before.   30

                            Wil. Rowley.

VERSES] Ford was later to commend plays by Massinger, Shirley, and Broome, but Middleton and Rowley never performed this service for another fellow playwright.

19–21.] 'To Tragedy: As light from darkness springs at the Thunderer's stroke, / May she, bringing ruin to the wicked, bring life to famous poets'; i.e. 'Tragedy brings its wicked characters to destruction and gives an ever-living fame to its dramatists'. The latter sentiment is much the same as that of the last line of Ford's commendation, and was a common compliment to poets.

22. *Middletonus*] Thomas Middleton (*c.* 1580–1627) collaborated with Webster during their earlier days and again for *Anything for a Quiet Life*, performed by the King's Men in 1621. He was appointed City Chronicler, 6 September 1620.

23. Poeta . . . Londinensis] poet and chronicler of London.

26. *bodied*] embodied, given form.

27. *answered*] justified.

28. *Her*] i.e. which her.

prove] prove it to be.

31. Rowley] actor and dramatist (*c.* 1585–1626); he was a frequent collaborator in writing plays, doing so with numerous writers, including Webster, Middleton, and Ford on different occasions in the 1620s.

To the reader of the author, and his *Duchess of Malfi*.

> Crown him a poet, whom nor Rome nor Greece
> Transcend in all theirs, for a masterpiece;
> In which, whiles words and matter change, and men   35
> Act one another, he, from whose clear pen
> They all took life, to memory hath lent
> A lasting fame, to raise his monument.
>
> *John Ford.*

35–6. *whiles . . . another*] i.e. 'while literature has its fashions and theatre continues to exist'; *words and matter* was a common phrase, opposing the style and substance (or content) of writing.

36. *clear*] pure, illustrious.

37. *all*] i.e. words, substance, and character.

39. John Ford] dramatist (?1586–1640) who may, like Webster, have started to write under Dekker's tutelage; he collaborated with Webster (and Dekker and Rowley) in the lost *Late Murder in Whitechapel* (1624).

The Actors' Names

[as given in the first edition]

Bosola, *J. Lowin.*
Ferdinand, 1. *R. Burbidge.* 2. *J. Taylor.*
Cardinal, 1. *H. Cundaile.* 2. *R. Robinson.*
Antonio, 1. *W. Ostler.* 2. *R. Benfield.*
Delio, *J. Underwood.*   5
Forobosco, *N. Towley.*
Malateste.
The Marquis of Pescara, *J. Rice.*
Silvio, *T. Pollard.*
The several madmen, *N. Towley, J. Underwood, etc.*   10
The Duchess, *R. Sharpe.*
The Cardinal's Mistress, *J. Tomson.*
The Doctor, ⎱ *R. Pallant.*
Cariola,   ⎰
Court Officers.   15
Three young children.
Two Pilgrims.

The Actors' Names] *The Duchess* is the earliest English play to be published with a list of actors assigned to individual roles; for the casting, see Introduction, pp. 22–3.

1.] In lists of characters prefixed to plays at this time, characters were placed in order of rank and status, the males first; Bosola has been given unprecedented prominence at the head of the cast-list. Webster may have been responsible for this (see Introduction, p. 30), thus expressing his view of the play's structure and the significance of its characters.

6. *Forobosco*] a 'ghost' character, mentioned in the dialogue, but not appearing on stage; see II.ii.32, note.

13–14.] The bracket was misplaced in Q, assigning Pallant the impossible task of playing Cariola and all the Court Officers.

[DRAMATIS PERSONAE

FERDINAND, *Duke of Calabria, twin brother to the Duchess.*
The Cardinal, *their brother.*
DANIEL DE BOSOLA, *returned from imprisonment in the galleys following service for the Cardinal; later the Provisor of Horse to the Duchess, and in the pay of Ferdinand.*
ANTONIO BOLOGNA, *Steward of the Household to the Duchess; later her husband.*
DELIO, *his friend; a courtier.*
CASTRUCHIO, *an old lord; husband of Julia.*
Marquis of PESCARA, *a soldier.*
Count MALATESTE, *a courtier at Rome.*
SILVIO, *a courtier at Malfi and Rome.*
RODERIGO ⎱ *courtiers at Malfi.*
GRISOLAN ⎰
Doctor.

The Duchess of Malfi, *a young widow; later wife of Antonio; sister to the Cardinal and twin sister to Ferdinand.*
CARIOLA, *her waiting-woman.*
JULIA, *wife of Castruchio and mistress of the Cardinal.*
Old Lady, *a midwife.*

Two Pilgrims.
Eight Madmen, *being an Astrologer, Lawyer, Priest, Doctor, English Tailor, Gentleman Usher, Farmer, and Broker.*
Court Officers; Servants; Guards; Executioners; Attendants; Churchmen.
Ladies-in-Waiting.

SCENE: *Malfi, Rome, Loretto, the countryside near Ancona, and Milan.*]

The Duchess of Malfi

Act I

Scene i

Enter ANTONIO *and* DELIO.

Delio. You are welcome to your country, dear Antonio;
    You have been long in France, and you return
    A very formal Frenchman in your habit.
    How do you like the French court?
Antonio.   I admire it—
    In seeking to reduce both state and people   5
    To a fixed order, their judicious king
    Begins at home: quits first his royal palace
    Of flatt'ring sycophants, of dissolute
    And infamous persons, which he sweetly terms
    His master's masterpiece, the work of heaven,   10
    Consid'ring duly that a prince's court
    Is like a common fountain, whence should flow
    Pure silver drops in general; but if 't chance
    Some cursed example poison 't near the head,

    I.i.0.1.] The location is the presence chamber in the Duchess's palace;
with a few important exceptions, the first four Acts are set somewhere in or
near this fortified palace and home.
    3. *habit*] dress.
    5. *reduce*] bring, restore.
    state and people] rulers and ruled, senate and general population.
    6. *fixed order*] propriety, regular and established rule.
    7. *quits*] rids.
    8. *sycophants*] parasites, tale-bearers.
    9. *infamous*] notoriously evil, shameful.
    12. *common*] shared by all.
    fountain] spring of water.
    13. *silver*] glittering, precious (poetic).
    in general] to everyone.
    14. *example*] person or persons for others to imitate.
    head] (1) source (of *fountain*, l. 12); (2) chief person, ruler.

Death and diseases through the whole land spread. 15
And what is 't makes this blessèd government
But a most provident council, who dare freely
Inform him the corruption of the times?
Though some o'th' court hold it presumption
To instruct princes what they ought to do, 20
It is a noble duty to inform them
What they ought to foresee.

Enter BOSOLA.

Here comes Bosola,
The only court-gall:—yet I observe his railing
Is not for simple love of piety;
Indeed he rails at those things which he wants, 25
Would be as lecherous, covetous, or proud,
Bloody, or envious, as any man,
If he had means to be so.

Enter Cardinal.

Here's the Cardinal.
Bosola. I do haunt you still.
Cardinal.   So.
Bosola.   I have done you
Better service than to be slighted thus. 30
Miserable age, where only the reward
Of doing well is the doing of it.
Cardinal. You enforce your merit too much.
Bosola. I fell into the galleys in your service, where, for two
years together, I wore two towels instead of a shirt, with 35

---

17. *provident*] foreseeing (see l. 22, below).
18. *Inform him*] keep him informed about.
19. *hold*] consider.
23. *court-gall*] scourge, or bitter satirist, of the court.
27. *envious*] malicious.
29. *haunt*] follow after, search for.
still] always, ever.
31. *only the reward*] the only reward.
33. *enforce*] stress, press (for attention).
34. *I . . . service*] i.e. what you asked me to do was punishable with imprisonment in the slave-ships.
35-7. *I . . . mantle*] With bitter sarcasm, Bosola gives mock dignity to poverty and hardship.

a knot on the shoulder, after the fashion of a Roman
mantle. Slighted thus? I will thrive some way: blackbirds
fatten best in hard weather; why not I, in these dog-days?
Cardinal. Would you could become honest.
Bosola. With all your divinity, do but direct me the way to it.   40
[*Exit* Cardinal.] I have known many travel far for it, and
yet return as arrant knaves as they went forth, because
they carried themselves always along with them.—Are
you gone? Some fellows, they say, are possessed with the
devil, but this great fellow were able to possess the great-   45
est devil, and make him worse.
Antonio. He hath denied thee some suit?
Bosola. He and his brother are like plum trees that grow
crooked over standing pools; they are rich and o'erladen
with fruit, but none but crows, pies, and caterpillars feed   50
on them. Could I be one of their flattering panders, I
would hang on their ears like a horse-leech till I were full,
and then drop off.—I pray, leave me.
     Who would rely upon these miserable dependences, in
expectation to be advanced tomorrow? What creature   55

---

37. *Slighted thus?*] The Cardinal may have walked or turned away; or
Bosola is so caught up in what he wants to say that he delays until now his
reply to line 33.

37–8. *blackbirds . . . weather*] i.e. by ruffling up their feathers, they *look* as
if they are well fed; since this is generally true of all small birds, Bosola may
use *black* to represent his ill-fortune.

38. *dog-days*] hottest and most unwholesome time of the year; usually
reckoned as the forty days following 11 August, when the sun is near Sirius,
the dog-star.

41 S.D.] In the absence of a direction in Q, an early exit is marked here,
so that the Cardinal does not allow himself to seem dependent on Bosola; a
little later, 'Are you gone' shows that he has left the stage before the 'court-
gall' can notice (see note, l. 37, above, for another indication of Bosola's
apparently self-absorbed railing or soliloquizing).

47. *suit*] petition.

49. *standing*] stagnant.

50. *crows . . . caterpillars*] Used frequently of inhuman men, these animals
represent appetite and need for dead flesh, cunning and deceit (mag*pies*),
and rapacious greed.

51. *panders*] used generally, not only with reference to sexual gratification.

52. *hang . . . ears*] (1) attach myself to them; (2) listen to their every word.
horse-leech] i.e. blood-sucker.

54. *dependences*] positions of subjection; with a punning echo of *hang
on*.

ever fed worse than hoping Tantalus? Nor ever died any
man more fearfully than he that hoped for a pardon.
There are rewards for hawks and dogs, and whores, when
they have done us service; but for a soldier, that hazards
his limbs in a battle, nothing but a kind of geometry is his   60
last supportation.

Delio. Geometry?

Bosola. Ay, to hang in a fair pair of slings, take his latter swing
in the world upon an honourable pair of crutches, from
hospital to hospital. Fare ye well, sir. And yet do not you   65
scorn us, for places in the court are but like beds in the
hospital, where this man's head lies at that man's foot,
and so lower, and lower.   [*Exit.*]

Delio. I knew this fellow seven years in the galleys
For a notorious murder, and 'twas thought   70
The Cardinal suborned it: he was released
By the French general, Gaston de Foix,
When he recovered Naples.

Antonio.   'Tis great pity
He should be thus neglected; I have heard
He's very valiant. This foul melancholy   75

---

56. *Tantalus*] proverbial figure of a hoping and disappointed man. According to myth, he was punished in Hades by being placed in the middle of a lake of water which always receded when he tried to drink, near a tree with fruit that always eluded his grasp, and under a huge rock which threatened to fall on his head.

57. *hoped for a pardon*] i.e. was publicly executed, hoping for a last-minute reprieve.

58. *whores*] This edition supplies a word which appears to be missing in Q (the preceding *and* would otherwise be redundant and a gap left by the compositor otherwise unexplained). Webster used *rewards* (a technical term of hunting) of *whores* several times in *The White Devil*; *limbs* and *supportation* have associations more fitting for *whores* than for *hawks* and *dogs*.

60. *geometry*] 'Hang by geometry' was proverbial.

61. *supportation*] (1) bearing of expense (the primary sense); (2) physical propping up.

63. *swing*] (1) forced movement (as on *crutches*); (2) fling, pleasurable indulgence.

66. *scorn*] mock, laugh at.

71. *suborned*] arranged secretly.

72–3. *French . . . Naples*] a (jumbled) topical reference taken from Painter's *Palace of Pleasure. recovered* = delivered, relieved.

75. *melancholy*] both a mental disease and, in Webster's time, a fashionable affectation among well-educated and disaffected men (see l. 278, below).

Will poison all his goodness, for—I'll tell you—
If too immoderate sleep be truly said
To be an inward rust unto the soul,
It then doth follow want of action
Breeds all black malcontents, and their close rearing,   80
Like moths in cloth, do hurt for want of wearing.

Enter SILVIO, CASTRUCHIO, JULIA, RODERIGO,
and GRISOLAN.

Delio. The presence 'gins to fill: you promised me
    To make me the partaker of the natures
    Of some of your great courtiers.
Antonio.   The Lord Cardinal's
    And other strangers', that are now in court?   85
    I shall.

Enter FERDINAND.

            Here comes the great Calabrian duke.
Ferdinand. Who took the ring oftenest?
Silvio. Antonio Bologna, my lord.
Ferdinand. Our sister Duchess' great master of her house-
    hold? Give him the jewel.—When shall we leave this   90
    sportive action, and fall to action indeed?

---

79. *follow want*] follow that lack.

80. *black*] alluding to (1) 'black bile', the supposed cause of this mental disease, and (2) the colour of dress worn by those affecting melancholy.

close rearing] secret breeding or growth, with an allusion to the solitary habits of men affecting melancholy.

81.] Q marks a new scene following this line (and some modern editors follow), but to do so misrepresents what the dialogue and continuous action require. Q's entry-directions have generally been altered by the scribe, Ralph Crane, to conform with continental style (see Introduction, p. 30–1).

82. *presence*] presence chamber or hall, used for official court occasions.

83. *partaker*] sharer (in your understanding).

87. *ring*] Riding at the *ring*, to carry it away on a lance, was a sport in chivalric tournaments. Ferdinand speaks with unintentional irony, since Antonio takes the Duchess's 'ring' at ll. 404–15. This word is the first in a series of others which Webster used elsewhere with sexual overtones: *jewel, sportive, action, fall*. Ferdinand's sexual references become obvious at ll. 104–14.

89. *great*] chief.

90. *jewel*] i.e. prize.

90–1. *leave . . . indeed*] i.e. exchange chivalric (militaristic) entertainment for actual warfare.

Castruchio. Methinks, my lord, you should not desire to go to
  war in person.

Ferdinand. Now for some gravity.—Why, my lord?

Castruchio. It is fitting a soldier arise to be a prince, but not   95
  necessary a prince descend to be a captain.

Ferdinand. No?

Castruchio. No, my lord; he were far better do it by a deputy.

Ferdinand. Why should he not as well sleep, or eat, by a
  deputy? This might take idle, offensive, and base office   100
  from him, whereas the other deprives him of honour.

Castruchio. Believe my experience: that realm is never long in
  quiet where the ruler is a soldier.

Ferdinand. Thou told'st me thy wife could not endure
  fighting.   105

Castruchio. True, my lord.

Ferdinand. And of a jest she broke, of a captain she met full of
  wounds—I have forgot it.

Castruchio. She told him, my lord, he was a pitiful fellow, to
  lie, like the children of Israel, all in tents.   110

Ferdinand. Why, there's a wit were able to undo all the
  chirurgeons o' the city for, although gallants should quarrel, and had drawn their weapons, and were ready to go
  to it, yet her persuasions would make them put up.

Castruchio. That she would, my lord.   115

---

100. *office*] function.

105. *fighting*] with *double entendre*, implying that Castruchio's 'realm', or
marriage, is '*un*quiet'.

107. *broke*] cracked.

110. *children of Israel*] a reading suggested in the New Mermaid ed.; Q
reads 'Ismail', which would have been an unusual spelling for 'Ishmael'
(which many editions print here) and would have made Julia's joke too
obscure to be efficient. 'Ismael' could easily be a misreading of *Israel* in the
printer's copy or Webster's manuscript. The Old Testament on several
occasions reports that *the children of Israel* lived *in tents*, but not those of
Ishmael.

in tents] (1) in canvas shelters; (2) in surgical dressings; (3) intentions
(punningly).

111. *were*] that would be.

112. *chirurgeons*] surgeons.

112–14. *although . . . up*] with sexual *double entrendres*, especially on *drawn
their weapons*, *go to it*, and *put up*.

Ferdinand. How do you like my Spanish jennet?

Roderigo. He is all fire.

Ferdinand. I am of Pliny's opinion; I think he was begot by the
    wind; he runs as if he were ballasted with quicksilver.

Silvio. True, my lord, he reels from the tilt often.   120

Roderigo, Grisolan. Ha, ha, ha!

Ferdinand. Why do you laugh? Methinks you that are
    courtiers should be my touchwood, take fire when I give
    fire; that is, laugh when I laugh, were the subject never so
    witty.   125

Castruchio. True, my lord, I myself have heard a very good
    jest, and have scorned to seem to have so silly a wit as to
    understand it.

Ferdinand. But I can laugh at your fool, my lord.

Castruchio. He cannot speak, you know, but he makes faces—   130
    my lady cannot abide him.

Ferdinand. No?

Castruchio. Nor endure to be in merry company; for she says
    too much laughing, and too much company, fills her too
    full of the wrinkle.   135

Ferdinand. I would then have a mathematical instrument

---

116. *jennet*] a light, sporting horse (inappropriate to the old Castruchio).

118. *Pliny's opinion*] i.e. as found in his *Natural History* (first century A.D.; translated into English, 1601).

119. *ballasted with quicksilver*] an attempt at wordplay: the weights (that should handicap the horse) are *quick* and thus add to its speed. *Quicksilver* is mercury.

120. *he . . . tilt*] more wordplay: (1) *ballast* rights the *tilt* (as of a boat); (2) the horse jibs (in jousting), as though drunk.

121. They may laugh at a third and bawdy meaning of *tilt* = act of sexual intercourse. If Ferdinand silences them because of this, having spoken bawdily himself (see note l. 87, above), his abrupt reproof will imply that there is one rule for a prince and another for courtiers and that his sexual awareness is very private and/or unpredictable. However motivated, the reproof shows how the courtier's task of seeking a prince's favour is both difficult and precarious; subtleties of this sort are consonant with the 'slippery ice-pavements' (V.ii.332) at court shown elsewhere in this play.

123. *touchwood*] tinder.

124. *when I laugh*] i.e. and only then.

127–30. *so silly . . . faces*] Congenital imbeciles were kept as 'fools' in great households; Castruchio's was a dumb idiot.

made for her face, that she might not laugh out of compass.—I shall shortly visit you at Milan, Lord Silvio.

Silvio. Your grace shall arrive most welcome.

Ferdinand. You are a good horseman, Antonio; you have   140
excellent riders in France. What do you think of good
horsemanship?

Antonio. Nobly, my lord. As out of the Grecian horse issued
many famous princes, so, out of brave horsemanship
arise the first sparks of growing resolution, that raise the   145
mind to noble action.

Ferdinand. You have bespoke it worthily.

Enter Cardinal, Duchess, CARIOLA[, *with* Attendants].

Silvio. Your brother, the Lord Cardinal, and sister Duchess.

Cardinal. Are the galleys come about?

Grisolan. They are, my lord.   150

Ferdinand. Here's the Lord Silvio, is come to take his leave.

Delio. Now sir, your promise: what's that Cardinal?

I mean his temper? They say he's a brave fellow,

137–8. *out of compass*] immoderately, beyond due limits; with a pun on
compass as a 'mathematical instrument' (l. 136).

138. *I . . . Silvio*] Using a prince's privilege, Ferdinand makes an abrupt
change of subject (as at ll. 116, 140). Together with l. 151, below, this
announcement suggests a particular and private understanding, as if Silvio
had some importance for Ferdinand, perhaps as his paid follower or 'creature' (l. 287, below).

139.] i.e. everyone will be more than happy to welcome you, despite the
great expense of appropriate entertainment.

143. *the Grecian horse*] the huge wooden horse, full of soldiers, which the
Trojans were tricked into bringing within the besieged walls of their city, thus
losing the long war. Antonio may answer the apparently simple question in
this roundabout way in order to emphasize his own ingenuity and so recom-
mend himself to the prince. However, the common wordplay on *whores/horse*
might possibly be present here (continuing the earlier string of sexual innu-
endoes), and be Webster's way of suggesting the covert sexual potential of
both men and also, with dramatic irony, their instinctive rivalry.

149–50.] This exchange is never developed in narrative or in the relationship between the two men; it is a brief, but theatrically effective, device for
suggesting that many private intrigues are being attended to during the
public business and formalities of the court.

Are . . . about?] have the galleys reversed course?

153. *brave*] i.e. bold, extravagant, and sociable (notably unpriestlike, as
are the pursuits listed below).

Will play his five thousand crowns at tennis, dance,
Court ladies, and one that hath fought single combats.   155
Antonio. Some such flashes superficially hang on him, for
form, but observe his inward character: he is a melancholy churchman. The spring in his face is nothing but
the engendering of toads; where he is jealous of any man,
he lays worse plots for them than ever was imposed on   160
Hercules, for he strews in his way flatterers, panders,
intelligencers, atheists, and a thousand such political
monsters. He should have been Pope, but instead of
coming to it by the primitive decency of the church, he
did bestow bribes so largely, and so impudently, as if he   165
would have carried it away without heaven's knowledge.
Some good he hath done.
Delio. You have given too much of him: what's his brother?
Antonio. The Duke there? A most perverse and turbulent
nature:
What appears in him mirth is merely outside;   170
If he laugh heartily, it is to laugh

---

154. *Will*] who will.

tennis] i.e. 'real', or royal, tennis: a fashionable and exclusive sport (see *W.D.* II.i.182).

155. *single combats*] duels.

156. *flashes*] showy, youthful behaviour.

157. *form*] merely outward appearances.

157–8. *melancholy*] see note at l. 75, above.

158–9. *spring . . . toads*] This idea is clearer in George Chapman, *Bussy D'Ambois* (1604), from which Webster may have borrowed it: 'thy gall [bitterness] / Turns all thy blood to poison, which is cause / Of that toadpool that stands in thy complexion' (III.ii.363–5).

159. *jealous*] suspicious.

160–1. *imposed on Hercules*] Offered choice of a life of toil and glory or one of ease and enjoyment, Hercules chose the former, and subsequently, besides suffering from fits of insanity, submitted himself to undertake twelve 'labours' of great difficulty and danger.

162. *intelligencers*] informers, spies.

atheists] impious, wicked persons (commonly used in this general sense).

political] shrewd, scheming.

164. *by . . . church*] Popes were elected according to strict and ancient rules which guarded against undue lobbying (some of the procedures are staged and explained in *W.D.* IV.ii).

166. *carried it away*] won the day (a common phrase).

168. *given*] said.

All honesty out of fashion.

Delio.   Twins?

Antonio.   In quality:
He speaks with others' tongues, and hears men's suits
With others' ears; will seem to sleep o'th' bench
Only to entrap offenders in their answers;   175
Dooms men to death by information,
Rewards by hearsay.

Delio.   Then the law to him
Is like a foul black cobweb to a spider:
He makes it his dwelling and a prison
To entangle those shall feed him.

Antonio.   Most true: 180
He ne'er pays debts, unless they be shrewd turns,
And those he will confess that he doth owe.
Last, for his brother, there, the Cardinal:
They that do flatter him most say oracles
Hang at his lips; and verily I believe them,   185
For the devil speaks in them.
But for their sister, the right noble Duchess:
You never fixed your eye on three fair medals
Cast in one figure, of so different temper.
For her discourse, it is so full of rapture   190
You only will begin then to be sorry
When she doth end her speech, and wish, in wonder,
She held it less vainglory to talk much
Than you penance to hear her. Whilst she speaks,

---

172. *Twins?*] The two brothers and their sister are very alike in appearance
and age (see ll. 188–9, below). Ferdinand says, very explicitly, that it is he and
his sister who are twins (IV.ii.266).

173–4. *speaks . . . ears*] i.e. does not say what he thinks, and pays no regard
when asked for favours.

176. *information*] private intelligence; (mere) accusation.

177–80. *the law . . . him*] an adaptation of a common proverb, 'the law, like
a cobweb, traps the little and allows the great to escape'. The spider eating
its victims is Webster's addition.

181. *shrewd turns*] malicious injuries (the opposite to a 'good turn').

184–5. *oracles . . . lips*] wisest people listen closely to all he says.

189. *figure*] mould.

temper] temperament, with pun on the *temper*ing of metals.

193. *vainglory*] worthless, unwarranted pride.

194. *penance*] i.e. think it is something to suffer.

She throws upon a man so sweet a look   195
That it were able raise one to a galliard
That lay in a dead palsy, and to dote
On that sweet countenance. But in that look
There speaketh so divine a continence
As cuts off all lascivious and vain hope.   200
Her days are practised in such noble virtue
That sure her nights—nay more, her very sleeps—
Are more in heaven than other ladies' shrifts.
Let all sweet ladies break their flatt'ring glasses,
And dress themselves in her.

Delio.   Fie, Antonio,   205
You play the wire-drawer with her commendations.

Antonio. I'll case the picture up only thus much.
All her particular worth grows to this sum:
She stains the time past, lights the time to come.

Cariola. You must attend my lady, in the gallery,   210
Some half an hour hence.

Antonio. I shall.

Ferdinand. Sister, I have a suit to you.

Duchess.   To me, sir?

Ferdinand. A gentleman here, Daniel de Bosola;
One that was in the galleys.

Duchess.   Yes, I know him.   215

Ferdinand. A worthy fellow h' is; pray let me entreat for
The provisorship of your horse.

Duchess.   Your knowledge of him

---

196. *galliard*] lively dance (with high leaps).

197. *palsy*] paralysis.

198–9. *countenance . . . continence*] a quibble; these words, from the same Latin source, were not always distinguished in spelling in Webster's time.

202. *her very sleeps*] i.e. even her dreams.

203. *shrifts*] confessions of sins.

205. *dress . . . her*] i.e. use her as a model.

206. *play the wire-drawer*] spin out your words, make much of little.

207. *case*] close, cover.

209. *stains*] eclipses, puts in the shade.

210. *gallery*] room used for taking exercise or for displaying works of art.

213. *suit*] petition.

217. *provisorship*] office of manager.

Commends him and prefers him.
Ferdinand.   Call him hither.

                        [*Exit* Attendant.]

We now are upon parting; good Lord Silvio,
Do us commend to all our noble friends   220
At the leaguer.
Silvio.   Sir, I shall.
Duchess.   You are for Milan?
Silvio. I am.
Duchess. Bring the caroches: we'll bring you down to the
    haven.

        [*Exeunt all except* Cardinal *and* FERDINAND.]

Cardinal. Be sure you entertain that Bosola
    For your intelligence. I would not be seen in 't;   225
    And therefore many times I have slighted him
    When he did court our furtherance, as this morning.
Ferdinand. Antonio, the great master of her household,
    Had been far fitter.
Cardinal.   You are deceived in him,

              Enter BOSOLA.

His nature is too honest for such business.   230
He comes; I'll leave you.   [*Exit.*]
Bosola.   I was lured to you.

---

218. *Commends . . . him*] recommends him.

221. *leaguer*] military camp.

You . . . Milan?] assigned in Q to Ferdinand who already has this information; the Duchess's subsequent speech would be very abrupt if she had not
asked this question.

223. *caroches*] coaches (of a stately kind).

bring] accompany.

224–5. *entertain . . . intelligence*] take Bosola into your service as a spy or
informer.

227. *court our furtherance*] ask me for advancement (*our* is the 'royal plural',
regularly used by a prince to refer to himself).

229 S.D.] An early entry for Bosola while the talk is about Antonio (as in
this edition) serves to emphasize how the two courtiers are both candidates
for advancement; their rivalry is apparent in II.i.79–111 and II.iii.9–41.

231. *lured*] A hawk is enticed back to the hunter's wrist by a 'lure', a device
made of feathers which simulates the appearance of a small bird. Bosola may
imply that he has been summoned especially; however, he could also mean
that his dependence on Ferdinand was habitual (as when he told the Cardinal, 'I do haunt you still', at l. 29, above).

Ferdinand. My brother here, the Cardinal, could never
    Abide you.
Bosola.   Never since he was in my debt.
Ferdinand. May be some oblique character in your face
    Made him suspect you.
Bosola.   Doth he study physiognomy?   235
    There's no more credit to be given to th' face
    Than to a sick man's urine, which some call
    The physician's whore, because she cozens him.
    He did suspect me wrongfully.
Ferdinand.   For that
    You must give great men leave to take their times: 240
    Distrust doth cause us seldom be deceived.
    You see, the oft shaking of the cedar tree
    Fastens it more at root.
Bosola.   Yet take heed,
    For to suspect a friend unworthily
    Instructs him the next way to suspect you,   245
    And prompts him to deceive you.
Ferdinand.   There's gold.
Bosola.   So:
    What follows? Never rained such show'rs as these
    Without thunderbolts in the tail of them.
    Whose throat must I cut?

---

234. *oblique character*] sign of mental perverseness or moral impropriety.

237. *urine*] used to diagnose sickness.

238. *cozens*] deceives.

240. *great men*] Ferdinand refers to his princely position with a phrase commonly used at this time of men who wielded great power, whether inherited or gained by their own exertions or graft. Webster had used it significantly in *W.D.*, notably in Vittoria's last words: 'O happy they that never saw the court, / Nor ever knew great man but by report' (V.vi.261–2). This begins a series of recurrences in this play.

    take their times] choose when they act.

241.] a version of the proverb, 'He who trusts not is not deceived'.

242–3. *oft . . . root*] The usual proverb noted that small shrubs are safe when great trees are felled by a storm. A *cedar* was a symbol of royal greatness.

245. *Instructs . . . way*] tells him to take the earliest opportunity.

247–8.] an allusion to the shower of gold in which form Jupiter visited the imprisoned Danaë.

Ferdinand. Your inclination to shed blood rides post   250
    Before my occasion to use you. I give you that
    To live i'th' court here, and observe the Duchess,
    To note all the particulars of her haviour,
    What suitors do solicit her for marriage
    And whom she best affects. She's a young widow—   255
    I would not have her marry again.
Bosola.   No, sir?
Ferdinand. Do not you ask the reason: but be satisfied,
    I say I would not.
Bosola.   It seems you would create me
    One of your familiars.
Ferdinand.   Familiar! What's that?
Bosola. Why, a very quaint invisible devil, in flesh: 260
    An intelligencer.
Ferdinand.   Such a kind of thriving thing
    I would wish thee; and ere long thou mayst arrive
    At a higher place by 't.
Bosola.   Take your devils
    Which hell calls angels! These cursed gifts would make
    You a corrupter, me an impudent traitor,   265

---

250. *post*] in haste.

255. *affects*] likes.

257–8.] *Do not . . . not*] See Introduction and notes at ll. 87, 105, 121, and
143, above, for Ferdinand's secret compulsions. His abrupt reproof here can
be played in many ways, with more or less sign of inner tension; but even the
most self-controlled Ferdinand, talking so pointedly and defensively to a
man he is about to hire as a spy, is likely to cause both Bosola and the theatre
audience to speculate about his 'reason' and his motives, matters about
which he himself may well be unsure. What is certain is that Webster has
created a sense of mystery that leads an audience to expect that an explanation will be given later. Ferdinand's following speeches give further sugges-
tions of insecurity and inner conflict, especially when he jumps on Bosola's
'familiars'.

259. *familiars*] (1) members of a household; (2) intimate friends; (3) 'familiar spirits', supposed to attend at a 'witch's' call. Ferdinand seizes upon
this word, probably because the third of these meanings leads him to think
of his sister's sexual powers which he associates with witchcraft elsewhere
(see l. 310, below; and III.i.78, and III.ii.141).

260. *quaint*] skilful, cunning.

263–4. *devils . . . angels*] Gold coins, called 'nobles', had a figure of St
Michael stamped on them and so were often referred to as 'angels'.

265. *impudent*] shameless.

And should I take these they'd take me to hell.
Ferdinand. Sir, I'll take nothing from you that I have given:—
    There is a place that I procured for you
    This morning: the provisorship o'th' horse—
    Have you heard on 't?
Bosola.   No.
Ferdinand.   'Tis yours—is 't not worth thanks?   270
Bosola. I would have you curse yourself now, that your
        bounty,
    Which makes men truly noble, e'er should make
    Me a villain. O, that to avoid ingratitude
    For the good deed you have done me, I must do
    All the ill man can invent! Thus the devil   275
    Candies all sins o'er; and what heaven terms vile,
    That names he complimental.
Ferdinand.   Be yourself:
    Keep your old garb of melancholy; 'twill express
    You envy those that stand above your reach,
    Yet strive not to come near 'em. This will gain   280
    Access to private lodgings, where yourself
    May, like a politic dormouse—
Bosola.   As I have seen some
    Feed in a lord's dish, half asleep, not seeming
    To listen to any talk; and yet these rogues
    Have cut his throat in a dream. What's my place?   285
    The provisorship o'th' horse? Say then, my corruption
    Grew out of horse dung: I am your creature.

---

268. *place*] office (in the Duchess's court).
271. *bounty*] munificence. In tradition and sometimes in practice, a great lord was expected to show his goodness and bind his followers to him by giving largess; this duty had been one of the foundations of feudal society.
276. *Candies*] sugars.
277. *complimental*] i.e. a polite accomplishment, or refinement.
278. *garb*] style, outward bearing.
282. *politic*] crafty.
dormouse] according to Pliny (see note, l. 118, above) dormice 'renewed their age' every year by sleeping hidden away and secure all winter; with summer they would reappear, young and fresh again.
283. *Feed . . . dish*] i.e. dine at a lord's table (at his expense).
285. *in a dream*] i.e. when asleep.
287. *your creature*] (1) your paid servant; (2) one whose fortune you have created (and for whom you are responsible).

Ferdinand. Away!
Bosola. Let good men, for good deeds, covet good fame,
    Since place and riches oft are bribes of shame—   290
    Sometimes the devil doth preach.   *Exit.*

          [*Enter* Duchess *and* Cardinal.]

Cardinal. We are to part from you, and your own discretion
    Must now be your director.
Ferdinand.   You are a widow:
    You know already what man is, and therefore
    Let not youth, high promotion, eloquence—   295
Cardinal. No, nor anything without the addition, honour,
    Sway your high blood.
Ferdinand.   Marry! They are most luxurious

289–91.] Bosola's concluding 'sentence' (see Introduction) and his own mocking comment on it are probably spoken to the theatre audience (see also following note), alerting them to his awareness that he has chosen a shameful course. He will return to this idea; see, especially, V.v.103–5. Spoken to Ferdinand, these three lines would be a very odd way of thanking him or recommending his own trustworthiness; they might, however, be used to seal a pact between two men who know they are committed to an evil course. Line 291 is proverbial: e.g. 'the devil can cite scripture for his purpose'.

291 S.D.] Possibly Ferdinand should leave the stage on 'Away' (l. 288), to re-enter here with the Cardinal and Duchess; so the change of location to 'the gallery' (l. 210) would be clearly indicated to the audience. Such a staging would also: (1) suggest that the family conference is conducted in a less public place than the presence chamber of the first part of Act I; (2) avoid the possible awkwardness of Ferdinand suddenly breaking into intimate talk with his sister at l. 293 (the three could enter as if already talking together); (3) give Bosola a clear stage and the audience's concentrated attention for ll. 289–91. However, Q does not support this arrangement, because if Ralph Crane, who prepared the printer's copy, had found directions for such an exit and re-entry, he would normally have marked a new scene when the stage was clear after l. 291. In a Jacobean theatre, curtains of some kind could be closed in front of an inner stage either here or before Antonio's entry at l. 361, so concealing the thrones appropriate to the 'presence' and marking the change of place which is required by the text; these curtains could be the 'arras' of l. 357.

296. *addition*] title.

297. *high blood*] noble lineage; Ferdinand, however, takes *blood* = 'passion, sexual appetite'.

luxurious] lecherous, unchaste.

Will wed twice.
Cardinal.   O, fie!
Ferdinand.   Their livers are more spotted
     Than Laban's sheep.
Duchess.   Diamonds are of most value,
     They say, that have passed through most jewellers'
          hands.   300
Ferdinand. Whores, by that rule, are precious.
Duchess.   Will you hear me?
     I'll never marry.
Cardinal.   So most widows say;
     But commonly that motion lasts no longer
     Than the turning of an hour-glass; the funeral sermon
     And it end both together.
Ferdinand.   Now hear me.   305
     You live in a rank pasture here, i'th' court:
     There is a kind of honeydew that's deadly;
     'Twill poison your fame. Look to 't; be not cunning,
     For they whose faces do belie their hearts
     Are witches, ere they arrive at twenty years—   310
     Ay, and give the devil suck.
Duchess. This is terrible good counsel.
Ferdinand. Hypocrisy is woven of a fine small thread,
     Subtler than Vulcan's engine; yet, believe 't,

---

298. *Will*] who will.

O, fie!] The modern, half-humorous usage (which usually sounds quaint)
was unknown in Webster's time; *fie* expressed disgust and was a strong
reproach.

livers] The liver was thought to be the seat of violent passions.

298–9. *more . . . sheep*] The Biblical story (see Genesis, 30.31–43) tells
how, having seemed to ask little from Laban for his service (who in return
tried to trick him out of even that), Jacob managed Laban's flocks so that
sheep that were all one colour gave birth to the parti-coloured lambs which
were to be his portion, and so thrived 'exceedingly'.

303. *motion*] resolve.

307. *honeydew*] a sweet, sticky substance found on leaves, etc., being
excreted by aphids; formerly it was supposed to be a kind of dew.

308. *your fame*] (1) what people say about you; (2) the memorable achievements of your whole life (see the play's last words, V.v.120–1).

313. *Hypocrisy*] dissimulation, hiding the real self.

314. *Vulcan's engine*] the net in which Vulcan caught Mars and Venus in
adultery; *engine* = contrivance, device.

Your darkest actions—nay, your privat'st thoughts—   315
Will come to light.
Cardinal.   You may flatter yourself,
And take your own choice; privately be married
Under the eaves of night.
Ferdinand.   Think 't the best voyage
That e'er you made; like the irregular crab,
Which, though 't goes backward, thinks that it goes
    right   320
Because it goes its own way. But observe:
Such weddings may more properly be said
To be executed than celebrated.
Cardinal. The marriage night
Is the entrance into some prison.
Ferdinand.   And those joys,   325
Those lustful pleasures, are like heavy sleeps
Which do forerun man's mischief.
Cardinal.   Fare you well.
Wisdom begins at the end; remember it.   [*Exit.*]
Duchess. I think this speech between you both was studied,
It came so roundly off.
Ferdinand.   You are my sister—   330
This was my father's poniard. Do you see?
I'd be loth to see 't look rusty, 'cause 'twas his.
I would have you to give o'er these chargeable revels;

---

318. *eaves*] overhanging cover, shelter.

319–21. *like . . . way*] A crab's sidelong motion gave rise to the notion that
it looked one way and moved in another; the idea that it believes it is going
in the direction in which it faces may be Webster's invention.

323. *executed*] Meanings ranged from 'carried out' (practically or legally)
to 'put to death'; the wordplay turns on the meaning 'celebrated' (used of
ceremonies and rites).

328. *Wisdom . . . end*] The paradox was used as a proverb, counselling
prudence, and also as a *memento mori*, advising that each day should be lived
as if one's last.

329. *studied*] rehearsed beforehand.

330. *roundly*] (1) fluently; (2) bluntly, forcefully.

331. *poniard*] short stabbing weapon, dagger.

332. *look rusty*] as if not used or not ready for use; indirectly, Ferdinand is
threatening his sister's life.

333. *chargeable*] burdensome, costly.

A visor and a mask are whispering-rooms
That were ne'er built for goodness. Fare ye well——   335
And women like that part which, like the lamprey,
Hath ne'er a bone in 't.

Duchess.   Fie, sir!

Ferdinand.   Nay,
I mean the tongue: variety of courtship.
What cannot a neat knave with a smooth tale
Make a woman believe? Farewell, lusty widow.   [*Exit.*]   340

Duchess. Shall this move me? If all my royal kindred
Lay in my way unto this marriage,
I'd make them my low footsteps: and even now,
Even in this hate, as men in some great battles,
By apprehending danger, have achieved   345
Almost impossible actions—I have heard soldiers say
   so—
So I, through frights and threat'nings, will assay
This dangerous venture. Let old wives report
I winked and chose a husband.—Cariola,

[*Enter* CARIOLA.]

To thy known secrecy I have given up   350
More than my life—my fame.

Cariola.   Both shall be safe,

---

334. *whispering-rooms*] intimate, private chambers.

336. *lamprey*] an eel-like fish.

337. *Fie, sir!*] The Duchess assumes her brother is speaking of a penis (cf. 'that part', l. 336).

338. *variety of courtship*] i.e. the different ways 'the tongue' may be used.

339. *neat*] fine, elegant, careful (sometimes used derogatorily).

knave] male servant (usually young).

tale] with wordplay on a man's 'tail' or penis.

340. *lusty*] merry, vigorous, lustful.

343. *footsteps*] steps (as before an altar or throne), rungs of a ladder.

344. *in this hate*] in the face of (my brothers') hatred, aversion.

349. *I . . . chose*] i.e. I chose with my eyes shut; but to *wink* also meant 'to shut one's eyes to wrongdoing'.

349.1 S.D.] Some editions direct Cariola to enter with her mistress at l. 291, but the later entrance has the advantage of Ferdinand and the Duchess being alone when he says (ll. 330ff.) what he seems to have restrained until after the Cardinal's departure. It also allows Cariola, but not her mistress, to know that Antonio is waiting (see l. 356).

351. *fame*] reputation. See note l. 289, above.

For I'll conceal this secret from the world
As warily as those that trade in poison
Keep poison from their children.
Duchess.   Thy protestation
Is ingenious and hearty; I believe it.   355
Is Antonio come?
Cariola.   He attends you.
Duchess.   Good dear soul,
Leave me, but place thyself behind the arras,
Where thou mayst overhear us. Wish me good speed,
For I am going into a wilderness
Where I shall find nor path nor friendly clew   360
To be my guide.   [*Cariola withdraws behind the arras.*]

[*Enter* ANTONIO.]

I sent for you. Sit down:
Take pen and ink, and write. Are you ready?
Antonio.   Yes.
Duchess. What did I say?
Antonio.   That I should write somewhat.
Duchess. O, I remember.
After these triumphs and this large expense,   365
It's fit, like thrifty husbands, we inquire
What's laid up for tomorrow.

---

355. *ingenious*] intelligent, sagacious (in opposition to 'hearty'); but the word was often used for 'ingenuous', and this sense may be implied here.
   hearty] from the heart.
356. *attends you*] awaits your orders.
357. *arras*] tapestry hanging at some distance from a wall, or over an alcove or an entrance to a room.
358. *speed*] fortune, luck.
360. *clew*] perhaps a reference to the ball of thread whereby Theseus entered the Minotaur's labyrinth and destroyed it, so winning Ariadne for his bride.
361 S.D.] On entry Antonio does not know that Cariola is behind the arras (see ll. 476–7), and so she may hide herself very quickly here, leaving her mistress to open the door for him. This unusual occurrence, together with the fact that he finds the Duchess alone, would explain Antonio's initial silence.
365. *triumphs*] festivities.
366. *husbands*] husbandmen, heads of households (concerned with husbanding resources).
367. *laid up*] put away (in store).

Antonio. So please your beauteous excellence.
Duchess.   Beauteous?
    Indeed I thank you: I look young for your sake.
    You have ta'en my cares upon you.
Antonio.   I'll fetch your grace   370
    The particulars of your revenue and expense.
Duchess.   O, you are an upright treasurer. But you mistook,
    For when I said I meant to make inquiry
    What's laid up for tomorrow, I did mean
    What's laid up yonder for me.
Antonio.   Where?
Duchess.   In heaven.   375
    I am making my will (as 'tis fit princes should,
    In perfect memory), and, I pray sir, tell me,
    Were not one better make it smiling, thus,
    Than in deep groans and terrible ghastly looks,
    As if the gifts we parted with procured   380
    That violent distraction?
Antonio.   O, much better.
Duchess.   If I had a husband now, this care were quit;
    But I intend to make you overseer.
    What good deed shall we first remember? Say.
Antonio.   Begin with that first good deed began i'th' world   385
    After man's creation, the sacrament of marriage:
    I'd have you first provide for a good husband,
    Give him all.
Duchess.   All?
Antonio.   Yes, your excellent self.
Duchess.   In a winding sheet?
Antonio.   In a couple.

---

369. *for your sake*] (1) thanks to you; (2) for love of you.

380. *procured*] produced.

381. *distraction*] confusion, madness (in association with 'violent', the latter meaning is the more prominent).

382. *quit*] got rid of.

383. *overseer*] person appointed by a testator to supervise or assist the executors of the will.

387. *provide for*] supply, make provision for.

389. *In . . . sheet*] i.e. 'ready to accompany my dead husband to the grave'.
    couple] i.e. of sheets; with wordplay on its other meanings of 'wedlock' and 'copulation'.

Duchess. Saint Winifred, that were a strange will!   390
Antonio. 'Twere strange if there were no will in you
    To marry again.
Duchess.   What do you think of marriage?
Antonio. I take 't, as those that deny purgatory:
    It locally contains or heaven, or hell;
    There's no third place in 't.
Duchess.   How do you affect it?   395
Antonio. My banishment, feeding my melancholy,
    Would often reason thus—
Duchess.   Pray, let's hear it.
Antonio. Say a man never marry, nor have children,
    What takes that from him? Only the bare name
    Of being a father, or the weak delight   400
    To see the little wanton ride a-cock-horse
    Upon a painted stick, or hear him chatter
    Like a taught starling.
Duchess.   Fie, fie, what's all this?
    One of your eyes is bloodshot—use my ring to 't.
    They say 'tis very sovereign—'twas my wedding ring,   405
    And I did vow never to part with it
    But to my second husband.
Antonio. You have parted with it now.
Duchess. Yes, to help your eyesight.
Antonio. You have made me stark blind.   410
Duchess. How?
Antonio. There is a saucy and ambitious devil

---

390. *Saint Winifred*] a seventh-century Welsh saint. Caradoc ap Alauc, whose love she had refused, struck her head off, but she was restored to life by St Bruno, her mother's brother.

  391. *will*] desire, passion; with a quibble on its meaning = 'testament'.

  393. *deny*] refuse to accept the existence of.

  394. *or . . . or*] either . . . or.

  395. *affect*] fancy, feel towards.

  396. *feeding*] Physicians warned that melancholy would be intensified if the sufferer were solitary.

  401. *wanton*] rogue (an endearment).

  403. *taught*] Starlings were sometimes kept as caged pets.

  404. *use . . . to 't*] i.e. as a medicinal, lucky charm.

  405. *sovereign*] efficacious, powerful.

  412. *devil*] i.e. ready to tempt him.

    Is dancing in this circle.
Duchess.   Remove him.
Antonio.   How?
Duchess. There needs small conjuration, when your finger
    May do it: thus.—Is it fit?
                    [*She puts her ring upon his finger;*] *he kneels.*
Antonio.   What said you?
Duchess.   Sir,   415
    This goodly roof of yours is too low built;
    I cannot stand upright in 't, nor discourse,
    Without I raise it higher. Raise yourself,
    Or, if you please, my hand to help you: so. [*Raises him.*]
Antonio. Ambition, madam, is a great man's madness,   420
    That is not kept in chains and close-pent rooms,
    But in fair, lightsome lodgings, and is girt
    With the wild noise of prattling visitants,
    Which makes it lunatic, beyond all cure.
    Conceive not I am so stupid but I aim   425
    Whereto your favours tend; but he's a fool
    That, being a-cold, would thrust his hands i'th' fire
    To warm them.
Duchess.   So, now the ground's broke,
    You may discover what a wealthy mine
    I make you lord of.
Antonio.   O, my unworthiness!   430
Duchess. You were ill to sell yourself.
    This dark'ning of your worth is not like that
    Which tradesmen use i'th' city; their false lights
    Are to rid bad wares off. And I must tell you,

---

413. *dancing . . . circle*] Magicians were said to raise spirits within a magic circle; Antonio is talking of the wedding ring.

418. *Without*] unless.

421. *close-pent*] locked up, secret.

423. *prattling*] prating, engaged in small-talk (not necessarily implying childish chattering). Antonio pictures a great man surrounded by courtiers who appear to speak about nothing, but are hoping to forward their individual 'suits'.

425. *aim*] (1) guess; (2) take aim.

432. *dark'ning*] obscuring.

433–4. *their . . . off*] Tradesmen use deceptive methods (i.e. weak light) to illuminate their shoddy goods (so that their defects are not seen).

If you will know where breathes a complete man— 435
I speak it without flattery—turn your eyes
And progress through yourself.
Antonio. Were there nor heaven nor hell,
I should be honest: I have long served virtue,
And ne'er ta'en wages of her.
Duchess.   Now she pays it. 440
The misery of us that are born great—
We are forced to woo, because none dare woo us;
And as a tyrant doubles with his words,
And fearfully equivocates, so we
Are forced to express our violent passions 445
In riddles and in dreams, and leave the path
Of simple virtue, which was never made
To seem the thing it is not. Go, go brag
You have left me heartless—mine is in your bosom,
I hope 'twill multiply love there. You do tremble: 450
Make not your heart so dead a piece of flesh,
To fear more than to love me. Sir, be confident.
What is 't distracts you? This is flesh and blood, sir;
'Tis not the figure cut in alabaster
Kneels at my husband's tomb. Awake, awake, man! 455
I do here put off all vain ceremony,
And only do appear to you a young widow
That claims you for her husband and, like a widow,
I use but half a blush in 't.
Antonio.   Truth speak for me:
I will remain the constant sanctuary 460

[Right margin handwritten note: Stands up to her proffers]

---

435. *complete*] perfect, fully accomplished.

437. *progress*] make a royal progress, or journey in state; i.e. 'you are ruler of such a man'.

438. *nor . . . nor*] neither . . . nor.

440. *pays*] repays, rewards.

442. *woo . . . woo*] familiar wordplay on 'woe' (the Q spelling), introduced by 'misery' of the previous line.

443. *doubles with*] has two meanings in, deceives with.

444. *fearfully*] (1) terribly, frighteningly; (2) apprehensively.

455. *Kneels*] that kneels.

456. *vain*] worthless; i.e. of no use to me now.
ceremony] rites and rights of sovereignty.

Of your good name.
Duchess.   I thank you, gentle love,
    And, 'cause you shall not come to me in debt,
    Being now my steward, here upon your lips
    I sign your *Quietus est.*   [*Kisses him.*]
    This you should have begged now;   465
    I have seen children oft eat sweetments thus,
    As fearful to devour them too soon.
Antonio. But for your brothers?
Duchess.   Do not think of them;
    All discord, without this circumference,
    Is only to be pitied, and not feared.   470
    Yet, should they know it, time will easily
    Scatter the tempest.
Antonio.   These words should be mine,
    And all the parts you have spoke, if some part of it
    Would not have savoured flattery.
Duchess. Kneel.   [*Cariola comes from behind the arras.*]   475
Antonio. Hah?
Duchess. Be not amazed, this woman's of my counsel.
    I have heard lawyers say, a contract in a chamber
    Per verba de presenti is absolute marriage.   [*They kneel.*]

-----

464. Quietus est] 'He is discharged, or acquitted of payment due';
the phrase was also used of the 'release' of death, as in *Hamlet*, III.i.75. There
is a series of allusions to death in this duologue; see ll. 375–81, 389, 451,
454–5.

469. *without this circumference*] outside these bounds. (Either they are now
in each other's arms or the Duchess alludes to the marriage bonds signified
by the wedding ring.)

473. *parts*] 'part' in the same line suggests that this is used quibblingly: (1)
parts of speech (cf. 'words', l. 472); (2) matter, particulars; (3) roles (of a
play), as suitor, widow, prince.

479. Per . . . presenti] 'by speaking in each other's presence'. When a
couple declared that they were man and wife (with or without a witness, and
without a deposition in writing), they were legally married. The church's
official attitude was that such marriages were valid and binding, but also
sinful and forbidden; offenders had to solemnize their marriage *in facie
ecclesiae*. The consummation of such unions before public solemnizing was
regarded as fornication and a deadly sin. In practice, however, sexual intercourse before the final religious ceremony was accepted behaviour for these
couples, despite the disapproval of Puritans and some clergy.

Bless, heaven, this sacred Gordian, which let violence   480
   Never untwine.
Antonio. And may our sweet affections, like the spheres,
   Be still in motion.
Duchess.   Quickening, and make
   The like soft music.
Antonio. That we may imitate the loving palms,   485
   Best emblem of a peaceful marriage,
   That ne'er bore fruit divided.
Duchess. What can the church force more?
Antonio. That Fortune may not know an accident,
   Either of joy or sorrow, to divide   490
   Our fixèd wishes.
Duchess.   How can the church bind faster?
   We now are man and wife, and 'tis the church
   That must but echo this.—Maid, stand apart.—

---

480. *heaven*] Censorship has probably altered an original 'God', here as elsewhere (see Introduction, p. 31).

Gordian] Gordius, King of Gordium in Phrygia, tied a knot in the yoke of oxen that pulled his chariot when he was chosen king. The oracle declared that whoever loosened it would rule Asia—which is what happened after Alexander the Great cut through the knot with his sword.

482–4.] The spheres, in which the planets were thought to move around the earth, were said to make continuous movement (*still* = constantly) and so interacted that they made music (*quickening* = stimulating, exciting) which could not be heard by mortal ears (*soft* = quiet, gentle). Between them, the Duchess and Antonio imagine their marriage being blessed with mutual and active pleasures, so that it is constant, heavenly, harmonious, and unknown to other people.

483. *still*] always.

485–7.] Another comparison that Webster could have taken from Pliny's *Natural History* (see note l. 118, above). A lone palm tree bears no fruit.

485, 489. *That*] Antonio (but no longer the Duchess) is praying to 'heaven' (l. 480), introducing new petitions with *That* in the manner of the Litany of the Church of England.

488. *force*] enforce (of a law or regulation); or, possibly, 'urge, require'.

491. *bind*] an emendation of Q which reads 'build'; this would have little or no meaning in the context, whereas *bind* is in keeping with 'contract . . . Gordian . . . like . . . divided . . . divide . . . faster . . . man and wife'. A compositor could easily mistake the two words in his copy, each with three or four strokes of the pen between 'b' and 'd'.

faster] more firmly.

I now am blind.

Antonio.   What's your conceit in this?

Duchess. I would have you lead your fortune by the hand,   495
    Unto your marriage bed.

    You speak in me this, for we now are one.

    We'll only lie, and talk together, and plot

    T'appease my humorous kindred; and, if you please,

    Like the old tale, in 'Alexander and Lodowick',   500

    Lay a naked sword between us, keep us chaste.—

    O, let me shroud my blushes in your bosom,

    Since 'tis the treasury of all my secrets.

                      [*Exeunt* Duchess *and* ANTONIO.]

---

494. *blind*] as Fortune (see ll. 489 and 495, in the second of which the meaning seems to be 'good fortune').

conceit] idea, fancy.

496.] The incomplete verse-line suggests a silence in which Antonio takes the Duchess in his arms. However, it would be possible for him to hesitate and remain kneeling, or at least apart from his wife, until after the very last word she speaks in this scene.

497.] with an echo of Antonio's concern about fulfilling his male role in courtship, as expressed in ll. 472–4.

499. *humorous*] ill-humoured; and possibly, with irony, 'capricious'.

500–1.] The story is found in a ballad to the tune of *Flying Fame: The Two Faithful Friends*. It tells how 'Alexander and Lodwick . . . were so like one another that none could know them asunder . . . how Lodowick married the Princess of Hungaria in Alexander's name and how each night he laid a naked sword between him and the Princess, because he would not wrong his friend'. The Duchess may propose such an action as a means of overcoming Antonio's fears; but her motives remain obscure, at least until the text is performed, at which time the actors can clarify what happens as they find how best they can act it. These lines can express the Duchess's own fears (see the next two lines), or her instinctive and irrational thoughts which may be about her brother (who is as like her as Lodowick is to Alexander; see note to l. 172, above), or about her father's poniard that Ferdinand has just shown her (see ll. 331–2, above).

502. *shroud*] conceal.

503.1 S.D.] Since Antonio leaves without saying a further word, a great freedom is allowed to the actors in showing the characters' mutual feelings and physical relationship at this moment. Perhaps the clearest clue to what Webster imagined is Cariola's recognition of what seems—from her point of view—to be *madness* in the Duchess's behaviour; certainly the frequently changing thoughts, rhythms, and modes of address in her mistress's words do not suggest any great confidence or stability. Antonio is a complete cipher on the page, and it is possible, but not easy, to play him that way on the stage.

Cariola. Whether the spirit of greatness or of woman
    Reign most in her, I know not, but it shows   505
    A fearful madness. I owe her much of pity.   *Exit.*

---

    504. *spirit . . . woman*] Cariola does not see the spirit of a great woman in
the Duchess but, rather, two qualities of almost equal power, that of a 'great
man' (see l. 240 and note, above) and that of a woman; her words seem to
imply that they are in opposition to each other.
    505–6. *shows . . . madness*] either 'the madness is terrible to witness' or 'the
madness appears to be the result of the Duchess's fears'.

Act II

Scene i

Enter BOSOLA *and* CASTRUCHIO.

Bosola. You say you would fain be taken for an eminent
    courtier?
Castruchio. 'Tis the very main of my ambition.
Bosola. Let me see, you have a reasonable good face for 't
    already, and your nightcap expresses your ears sufficient   5
    largely. I would have you learn to twirl the strings of your
    band with a good grace, and in a set speech, at th' end of
    every sentence, to hum three or four times, or blow your
    nose till it smart again, to recover your memory. When
    you come to be a president in criminal causes, if you   10
    smile upon a prisoner, hang him, but if you frown upon

II.i.0.1.] Early entries without specific motivation, talk of the court as if
everyone is waiting for something to happen, Bosola's bringing of a gift in
expectation of presenting it, the Duchess's address to Antonio and Bosola as
if she expected them to be in attendance, and her reference to etiquette and
'the presence' (l. 124) all show that the location for this scene is, once more,
the presence chamber of the Duchess's palace.

    1. *fain be*] be glad to be.

    2. *courtier*] member of a law court. Bosola uses the word in this unusual
sense, to mock the old man's presence among the young and hopeful *courtiers*
of the Duchess's entourage.

    3. *main*] aim, purpose, main part.

    5–6. *your nightcap . . . largely*] your donkey's ears (i.e. stupidity) are
pushed out amply enough by your lawyer's coif. Jokes about nightcaps are
usually aimed at cuckolds (see, for example, *W.D.*, I.ii.87–9), but, since the
rest of this speech is about Castruchio's activities as a lawyer, Bosola is
referring primarily to a lawyer's skull-cap and only secondarily to the old
man's lack of virility.

    7. *band*] neck-band, worn by lawyers and also, in elaborate varieties, by
men of fashion. They featured *strings* or white tabs.

    9. *to . . . memory*] Bosola mocks him as an old, bumbling lawyer, at a loss
for words.

    10. *president*] presiding judge.

him and threaten him, let him be sure to 'scape the
gallows.

Castruchio. I would be a very merry president.

Bosola. Do not sup o' nights; 'twill beget you an admirable   15
wit.

Castruchio. Rather it would make me have a good stomach to
quarrel, for they say your roaring boys eat meat seldom,
and that makes them so valiant. But how shall I know
whether the people take me for an eminent fellow?   20

Bosola. I will teach a trick to know it: give out you lie a-dying,
and if you hear the common people curse you, be sure
you are taken for one of the prime nightcaps.

Enter an Old Lady.

You come from painting now?

Old Lady. From what?   25

Bosola. Why, from your scurvy face-physic. To behold thee
not painted inclines somewhat near a miracle: these, in
thy face here, were deep ruts and foul sloughs the last
progress. There was a lady in France that, having had the
smallpox, flayed the skin off her face to make it more   30
level; and, whereas before she looked like a nutmeg-
grater, after she resembled an abortive hedgehog.

Old Lady. Do you call this painting?

Bosola. No, no, but careening of an old morphewed lady, to

---

17. *stomach*] (1) appetite; (2) anger.

18. *roaring boys*] wild, young trouble-makers.

20. *an eminent fellow*] one capable of good companionship.

23. *nightcaps*] lawyers (an allusion to their head-caps; see note, ll. 5–6,
above).

23 S.D.] The Old Lady's entry is unexplained here; but she has private
business which will become clear when she returns as a midwife in the next
scene.

26. *scurvy face-physic*] contemptible face-painting.

28. *sloughs*] muddy ditches, i.e. layers of dead skin.

29. *progress*] state journey or visitation made by a monarch, an occasion for
ostentatious display.

34. *but*] only. Q reads 'but you call' which is obviously wrong; some
editions read 'but I call it'.

34–5. *careening . . . again*] i.e. scraping clean an old scurfy lady, as if she
were the hull of a ship, so that she can look for new adventures, like a ship
putting to sea again.

make her disembogue again. There's roughcast phrase to   35
your plastic.

Old Lady. It seems you are well acquainted with my closet.

Bosola. One would suspect it for a shop of witchcraft, to find
in it the fat of serpents, spawn of snakes, Jews' spittle, and
their young children's ordure—and all these for the face.   40
I would sooner eat a dead pigeon, taken from the soles of
the feet of one sick of the plague, than kiss one of you
fasting. Here are two of you whose sin of your youth is the
very patrimony of the physician, makes him renew his
footcloth with the spring and change his high-prized   45
courtesan with the fall of the leaf: I do wonder you do not
loathe yourselves. Observe my meditation now:
What thing is in this outward form of man
To be beloved? We account it ominous
If nature do produce a colt, or lamb,   50
A fawn, or goat, in any limb resembling
A man, and fly from 't as a prodigy.
Man stands amazed to see his deformity
In any other creature but himself.
But in our own flesh, though we bear diseases   55
Which have their true names only ta'en from beasts,

35–6. *roughcast . . . plastic*] coarse (harsh, brutal) plaster as language to
describe your fine, artistic modelling, your face-painting.

40. *ordure*] excrement.

41–2. *dead . . . plague*] A recommended cure for plague was for the bared
rump of a bird to be held to the plague sore until the creature died from the
poison this drew from the sufferer's heart; the procedure was to be repeated
until all the poison has been drawn forth and no more deaths occurred.

43. *fasting*] i.e. when the woman's breath would be foul, in the morning.

43–4. *whose . . . physician*] i.e. you who are so riddled with venereal diseases and other ill effects of youthful indulgence that you must pay your
physicians huge fortunes in a search for cures.

45. *footcloth*] a rich cloth laid over the back of a horse to protect the rider
from mud and dust. It was a sign of wealth and dignity. The physician will
be so wealthy that be will be able to get a new footcloth every spring and a
new courtesan every autumn.

47. *Observe my meditation*] pay attention to the words that guide my act of
meditation.

48. *form*] appearance.

As the most ulcerous wolf and swinish measle,
Though we are eaten up of lice and worms,
And though continually we bear about us
A rotten and dead body, we delight   60
To hide it in rich tissue. All our fear—
Nay, all our terror—is lest our physician
Should put us in the ground, to be made sweet.—
Your wife's gone to Rome; you two couple, and get you
to the wells at Lucca, to recover your aches.   65
                    [*Exeunt* CASTRUCHIO *and* Old Lady.]
I have other work on foot. I observe our Duchess
Is sick o' days, she pukes, her stomach seethes,
The fins of her eyelids look most teeming blue,
She wanes i'th' cheek, and waxes fat i'th' flank,
And (contrary to our Italian fashion)   70
Wears a loose-bodied gown—there's somewhat in 't!
I have a trick may chance discover it,
A pretty one: I have bought some apricocks,
The first our spring yields.

                    Enter ANTONIO *and* DELIO[, *talking apart*].

Delio.   And so long since married?
    You amaze me.
Antonio.   Let me seal your lips for ever,   75
    For, did I think that anything but th' air
    Could carry these words from you, I should wish

---

57. *wolf*] Lupus (wolf) is a medical term for ulcers and cancerous growths.
swinish measle] The common human disease of measles (formerly the singular form was used) is here linked with a skin disease in swine; both were also confused with 'mesel', or leprosy.

60. *dead*] i.e. dying.

61. *tissue*] fine, delicate cloth.

65. *Lucca*] a famous spa in the sixteenth and seventeenth centuries.

68. *fins*] fish-like skins.
teeming] fruitful, as in pregnancy.

71. *loose-bodied*] In Webster's England, loose, unwaisted gowns were worn by older women.
there's . . . in 't] (1) something is going on; (2) there's something under her gown.

You had no breath at all.

[*To Bosola*] Now, sir, in your contemplation? You are
studying to become a great wise fellow?   80

Bosola. O, sir, the opinion of wisdom is a foul tetter that runs
all over a man's body. If simplicity direct us to have no
evil, it directs us to a happy being; for the subtlest folly
proceeds from the subtlest wisdom. Let me be simply
honest.   85

Antonio. I do understand your inside.

Bosola. Do you so?

Antonio. Because you would not seem to appear to the world
puffed up with your preferment, you continue this out-
of-fashion melancholy. Leave it, leave it.   90

Bosola. Give me leave to be honest in any phrase, in any
compliment whatsoever. Shall I confess myself to you? I
look no higher than I can reach: they are the gods that
must ride on winged horses; a lawyer's mule of a slow
pace will both suit my disposition and business. For mark   95
me, when a man's mind rides faster than his horse can
gallop, they quickly both tire.

Antonio. You would look up to heaven, but I think
The devil, that rules i'th' air, stands in your light.

79–111.] This small talk while waiting for the Duchess's entry—
opinionated, ironic, and complimentary—shows two ambitious men sparring
for advantage: Bosola out-plays Antonio by pretending at one point to reveal
all (l. 92) and then turning defence into attack.

81. *the opinion of wisdom*] a reputation for being wise.

tetter] sore.

82–3. *If . . . evil*] i.e. if we are not wise, or clever, enough to see how to do
evil.

83–4. *for . . . wisdom*] i.e. for we can be too wise or clever for our own
good, so that we are stupid in the most complicated way.

86. *inside*] i.e. what you hide about yourself.

89–90. *out-of-fashion melancholy*] See I.i.75 and 278–82, and notes.
Bosola's *melancholy* is *out-of-fashion* now because he has got preferment as
Provisor of the Horse.

94. *mule*] proverbially a stupid and slow animal.

95–7. *mark me . . . tire*] Bosola may well be alluding to Antonio's prowess
in horsemanship, which was given the prize and highly praised at the beginning of the play.

99. *devil . . . air*] Biblical: Ephesians, 2.2.

Bosola. O, sir, you are lord of the ascendant, chief man with			100
the Duchess; a duke was your cousin-german removed.
Say you were lineally descended from King Pepin, or he
himself, what of this? Search the heads of the greatest
rivers in the world, you shall find them but bubbles of
water. Some would think the souls of princes were			105
brought forth by some more weighty cause than those of
meaner persons—they are deceived; there's the same
hand to them: the like passions sway them, the same
reason that makes a vicar go to law for a tithe-pig and
undo his neighbours makes them spoil a whole province			110
and batter down goodly cities with the cannon.

Enter Duchess [*with* Attendants *and* Ladies].

Duchess. Your arm, Antonio—do I not grow fat?
I am exceeding short-winded.—Bosola,
I would have you, sir, provide for me a litter,
Such a one as the Duchess of Florence rode in.			115
Bosola. The Duchess used one when she was great with child.
Duchess. I think she did.—Come higher; mend my ruff.
Here. When? Thou art such a tedious lady, and

---

100. *lord of the ascendant*] Astrologers divided the heavens into twelve
'houses'; the 'first house', or 'house of *the ascendant*', is that section of the sky
which, at the beginning of a day, was thought to be rising in the east; the *lord
of the ascendant* was the planetary ruler of the ascending sign of the zodiac.
Bosola speaks with (unintentional) irony, since the *lord of the ascendant* was
supposed to have a special influence upon the life of a child born at that time.

101. *cousin-german removed*] first cousin once removed.

102. *King Pepin*] King of the Franks and founder of the Papal States, who
died in 768; in *W.D.*, Webster ranked him with the great rulers, Alexander
and Caesar (V.vi.108–12).

103. *Search the heads*] seek for, examine the sources.

106. *brought . . . cause*] brought about by a more important process, by
birth of greater consequence.

107. *meaner*] of lower social status.

107–8. *there's . . . them*] the same God moulded, created them.

109. *tithe-pig*] In rural areas, the tithe, or tenth part, of yearly earnings,
which was due to be given by parishioners to the vicar of their parish church,
was sometimes paid with farm produce rather than money.

110. *spoil*] plunder, lay waste.

114. *a litter*] a small enclosed carriage, borne on the shoulders of men or
animals.

118. *When?*] an exclamation of impatience.

tedious] troublesome, slow.

Thy breath smells of lemon peels. Would thou hadst
  done!
Shall I swoon under thy fingers? I am   120
So troubled with the mother.
Bosola. [*Aside*]   I fear too much.
Duchess. I have heard you say that the French courtiers
  Wear their hats on 'fore the king.
Antonio.   I have seen it.
Duchess. In the presence?
Antonio. Yes.
Duchess.   Why should not we bring up that fashion?   125
  'Tis ceremony more than duty that consists
  In the removing of a piece of felt.
  Be you the example to the rest o' th' court,
  Put on your hat first.
Antonio.   You must pardon me.
  I have seen, in colder countries than in France,   130
  Nobles stand bare to th' prince; and the distinction
  Methought showed reverently.
Bosola. I have a present for your grace.
Duchess.   For me, sir?
Bosola. Apricocks, madam.
Duchess.   O, sir, where are they?

---

119. *lemon peels*] kept in the mouth to hide a bad breath.

120. *swoon*] with 'under thy fingers', there may be wordplay on 'sound'
= 'making a sound' (as on a musical instrument); Q's 'sound' was a common
spelling for *swoon*.

121. *the mother*] hysteria. (The pun is common.)

122–3. *I . . . king*] an issue debated frequently at this time, when the
power of absolute monarchs was being modified by social and economic
changes. In its present context, this is neither casual nor wholly political talk;
the Duchess is teasing Antonio, and wants the private excitement of seeing
him with his hat on before the rest of the court remove theirs, as if he were
being acknowledged publicly as her husband. Antonio develops the secret
meanings by saying he has seen 'Nobles stand bare to th' prince' as, in
another sense, he has stood *bare*, or naked, before the Duchess, his 'prince'.
(At III.ii.5, she speaks of him as a 'nobleman'.)

131. *bare*] bare-headed.

134–5.] The phallic suggestiveness of *apricocks* (then a common form of
'apricots') may be one reason why the Duchess blushes immediately; Bosola
expresses delight because he has been waiting to see the effect of eating them
(see ll. 158–9). She also eats them 'greedily' (l. 151), so that in three ways his
'present' will provide Bosola with proof of her pregnancy.

I have heard of none to-year.

Bosola. [*Aside*]   Good, her colour rises.   135

Duchess. [*Taking the fruit*] Indeed, I thank you; they are won-
    drous fair ones.

    What an unskilful fellow is our gardener!

    We shall have none this month.   [*She eats.*]

Bosola. Will not your grace pare them?

Duchess. No, they taste of musk, methinks; indeed they do.   140

Bosola. I know not; yet I wish your grace had pared 'em.

Duchess. Why?

Bosola.   I forgot to tell you, the knave gard'ner,

    Only to raise his profit by them the sooner,

    Did ripen them in horse dung.

Duchess.   O, you jest!

    [*To Antonio*] You shall judge. Pray, taste one.

Antonio.   Indeed, madam,   145

    I do not love the fruit.

Duchess.   Sir, you are loth

    To rob us of our dainties. [*To Bosola*] 'Tis a delicate fruit;

    They say they are restorative.

Bosola.   'Tis a pretty art,

    This grafting.

Duchess.   'Tis so; a bett'ring of nature.

Bosola. To make a pippin grow upon a crab,   150

    A damson on a blackthorn. [*Aside*] How greedily she eats
    them!

    A whirlwind strike off these bawd farthingales,

    For, but for that and the loose-bodied gown,

    I should have discovered apparently

---

135. *to-year*] this year (as in 'today').

146-7. *you . . . dainties*] another, privately shared, *double entendre: dainties*
= (1) choice foods; (2) luxuries; (3) sexual pleasures.

149. *grafting*] placing a part of one tree into the living 'body' of another,
and so another word that can have sexual connotations. Unintentionally, but
perhaps catching the tone of what is being said, Bosola continues the innu-
endoes.

150. *a pippin . . . crab*] a sweet desert apple . . . a sour crab-apple tree.

151. *blackthorn*] a common or wild thorn tree, bearing very small black
fruit.

152. *bawd*] deceiving (for sexual or illicit purposes).

farthingales] frameworks of hoops, used to extend the skirts of dresses.

154. *apparently*] visibly.

The young springal cutting a caper in her belly.   155
Duchess. I thank you, Bosola, they were right good ones,
    If they do not make me sick.
Antonio.   How now, madam?
Duchess. This green fruit and my stomach are not friends.
    How they swell me!
Bosola. [*Aside*]   Nay, you are too much swelled already.
Duchess. O, I am in an extreme cold sweat!   160
Bosola. I am very sorry.
Duchess. Lights to my chamber! O good Antonio,
    I fear I am undone.   *Exit.*
Delio.   Lights there, lights!
        [*Exeunt all except* ANTONIO *and* DELIO.]
Antonio. O my most trusty Delio, we are lost!
    I fear she's fall'n in labour; and there's left   165
    No time for her remove.
Delio.   Have you prepared
    Those ladies to attend her, and procured
    That politic safe conveyance for the midwife
    Your duchess plotted?
Antonio. I have.
Delio.   Make use then of this forced occasion: 170
    Give out that Bosola hath poisoned her
    With these apricocks; that will give some colour
    For her keeping close.
Antonio.   Fie, fie, the physicians
    Will then flock to her.
Delio.   For that you may pretend
    She'll use some prepared antidote of her own,   175
    Lest the physicians should re-poison her.
Antonio. I am lost in amazement. I know not what to think
    on 't.   *Exeunt.*

---

155. *springal*] stripling.
cutting a caper] dancing merrily.
168. *politic*] cunning, carefully contrived.
conveyance] escort, means of entry.
170. *forced*] enforced, unsought.
172. *colour*] pretext.
173. *close*] private, secret.

Scene ii

Enter BOSOLA.

Bosola. So, so: there's no question but her tetchiness and
most vulturous eating of the apricocks are apparent signs
of breeding.—

Enter Old Lady.

Now?

Old Lady. I am in haste, sir.　　　　　　　　　　　　　　5

Bosola. There was a young waiting-woman had a monstrous
desire to see the glass-house.

Old Lady. Nay, pray let me go.

Bosola. And it was only to know what strange instrument it
was should swell up a glass to the fashion of a woman's　　10
belly.

Old Lady. I will hear no more of the glass-house—you are still
abusing women!

Bosola. Who, I? No, only (by the way now and then) mention
your frailties. The orange tree bears ripe and green fruit　　15
and blossoms all together; and some of you give entertainment for pure love, but more for more precious reward. The lusty spring smells well, but drooping autumn
tastes well. If we have the same golden showers that
rained in the time of Jupiter the Thunderer, you have the　　20
same Danaës still, to hold up their laps to receive them.—
Didst thou never study the mathematics?

II.ii.0.1.] The location remains the same as for the previous scene.

1. *tetchiness*] irritability, testiness.

2. *apparent*] obvious.

5.] The Old Lady is the midwife and may carry some parcel or bag which
will, incidentally, make this clear to Bosola and the audience.

7. *glass-house*] glass-factory. There was one near the Blackfriars Theatre,
where *The Duchess* was performed.

15. *your*] i.e. of you women in general.

15–21. *The orange . . . them*] i.e. some women make love in youth and for
pure love's sake; some, for gain; others, like the Old Lady, when they are
drooping.

21. *Danaës*] See I.i.247–8, note.

Old Lady. What's that, sir?

Bosola. Why, to know the trick how to make a many lines
    meet in one centre. Go, go, give your foster-daughters   25
    good counsel: tell them that the devil takes delight to
    hang at a woman's girdle, like a false, rusty watch, that
    she cannot discern how the time passes.

                                                 [Exit Old Lady.]

            Enter ANTONIO, DELIO, RODERIGO, GRISOLAN.

Antonio. Shut up the court gates.

Roderigo.   Why, sir? What's the danger?

Antonio. Shut up the posterns presently, and call   30
    All the officers o'th' court.

Grisolan.   I shall, instantly.   *[Exit.]*

Antonio. Who keeps the key o'th' park gate?

Roderigo.   Forobosco.

Antonio. Let him bring 't presently.

            Enter [GRISOLAN *with*] Officers.

First Officer. O, gentlemen o'th' court, the foulest treason!

Bosola. *[Aside]* If that these apricocks should be poisoned
    now,   35
    Without my knowledge!

First Officer. There was taken even now a Switzer in the
    Duchess' bed-chamber.

Second Officer. A Switzer?

First Officer. With a pistol in his great codpiece.   40

    24–5. *to know . . . centre*] In this sexual *double entendre*, the mathematical
image points to the woman's body, where all lines meet.

    30. *posterns*] small, back or side doors.

    presently] at once.

    32. *Forobosco*] The name does not appear elsewhere in the text of the play,
although it does in the list of Characters prefaced to Q (which also lists 'N.
Towley' or Tooley as performer of this role). Presumably Forobosco is the
name of one of the court 'Officers' (in this scene and III.ii) who are distinguished only by numbers elsewhere in the text; at some stage in the play's
composition he may have had a significantly individual role.

    37. *Switzer*] Swiss mercenary soldier; many found employment in the
feuds between Italian noblemen.

    40. *codpiece*] a necessary accessory to the close-fitting hose or breeches of
the period. Such pouches were often ornamented and enlarged, sometimes
so that they could hold a handkerchief or purse, or even oranges. They were
becoming old-fashioned by the end of the sixteenth century.

Bosola. Ha, ha, ha!

First Officer. The codpiece was the case for 't.

Second Officer. There was a cunning traitor. Who would have
    searched his codpiece?

First Officer. True, if he had kept out of the ladies' chambers.   45
    And all the moulds of his buttons were leaden bullets.

Second Officer. O, wicked cannibal! A fire-lock in 's codpiece!

First Officer. 'Twas a French plot, upon my life.

Second Officer. To see what the devil can do!

Antonio. All the officers here?   50

Officers. We are.

Antonio. Gentlemen,
    We have lost much plate, you know; and but this evening
    Jewels, to the value of four thousand ducats,
    Are missing in the Duchess' cabinet.   55
    Are the gates shut?

Officers.   Yes.

Antonio.   'Tis the Duchess' pleasure
    Each officer be locked into his chamber
    Till the sun-rising, and to send the keys
    Of all their chests and of their outward doors
    Into her bedchamber. She is very sick.   60

Roderigo. At her pleasure.

Antonio. She entreats you take 't not ill: the innocent
    Shall be the more approved by it.

Bosola. Gentleman o'th' woodyard, where's your Switzer
    now?   65

41.] bawdy laughter at the unintentional wordplay on *pistol* and pizzle
(= penis). The current colloquial pronunciation of *pistol* was without the
medial *t* (as in modern 'castle').

46. *moulds of*] shapes for; such *moulds* would be covered with cloth to hide
them from view. The *bullets* here suggest testicles.

47. *fire-lock*] firing-chamber of the pistol (having a further bawdy conno-
tation—testicles, as source of semen and/or sexual drive).

48. *French*] Among other attributes, the French were said to be courteous,
hasty, and lustful.

53. *plate*] money.
    but] only.

54. *ducats*] gold or silver coins.

55. *cabinet*] case for the safekeeping of valuables; private apartment.

63. *approved*] vindicated.

64. *woodyard*] yard where wood is cut and stored; an outlying and disrepu-
table part of Whitehall; used here to give the gentleman a mocking title.

First Officer. By this hand, 'twas credibly reported by one o'
   the black guard. [*Exeunt all except* ANTONIO *and* DELIO.]
Delio. How fares it with the Duchess?
Antonio.   She's exposed
   Unto the worst of torture, pain, and fear.
Delio. Speak to her all happy comfort.   70
Antonio. How I do play the fool with mine own danger!
   You are this night, dear friend, to post to Rome;
   My life lies in your service.
Delio.   Do not doubt me.
Antonio. O, 'tis far from me; and yet fear presents me
   Somewhat that looks like danger.
Delio.   Believe it,   75
   'Tis but the shadow of your fear, no more.
   How superstitiously we mind our evils!
   The throwing down salt, or crossing of a hare,
   Bleeding at nose, the stumbling of a horse,
   Or singing of a cricket, are of pow'r   80
   To daunt whole man in us. Sir, fare you well.
   I wish you all the joys of a blest father;
   And, for my faith, lay this unto your breast:
   Old friends, like old swords, still are trusted best.
                                     [*Exit.*]

Enter CARIOLA.

Cariola. Sir, you are the happy father of a son;   85
   Your wife commends him to you.
Antonio.   Blessed comfort!

---

67. *black guard*] lowest menials of a noble household.

72. *post*] speed (i.e. take *post*-horses).

73. *lies in*] depends upon.

75. *Somewhat*] some thing of unspecified or unknown nature.

76. *shadow*] imaginary image.

77. *mind*] think of, consider.

78. *crossing of a hare*] Coming across a hare boded either disordered senses
or the presence of a witch.

79–80. *stumbling . . . cricket*] Both were believed to bode death.

81. *whole man*] Cf. *W.D.*, I.i.45: 'Have a full man within you' (be fully
fortified and resolved).

83. *for my faith*] as for my loyalty, trustworthiness.

84.] a significant rephrasing of a proverb: 'Old friends and old wine are
best'.

For heaven sake, tend her well. I'll presently
Go set a figure for 's nativity.   *Exeunt.*

Scene iii

Enter BOSOLA[, *with a dark lantern*].

Bosola. Sure I did hear a woman shriek. List, hah?
    And the sound came, if I received it right,
    From the Duchess' lodgings. There's some stratagem
    In the confining all our courtiers
    To their several wards: I must have part of it;   5
    My intelligence will freeze else. List again!
    It may be 'twas the melancholy bird,
    Best friend of silence and of solitariness,
    The owl, that screamed so.

Enter ANTONIO.

                 Hah? Antonio!
Antonio. I heard some noise.—Who's there? What art thou?
    Speak.   10
Bosola. Antonio? Put not your face nor body
    To such a forced expression of fear—
    I am Bosola, your friend.
Antonio.   Bosola!
    [*Aside*] This mole does undermine me.
                           [*To him*] Heard you not

---

87. *presently*] immediately.
88. *Go . . . nativity*] go cast a horoscope, calculate the aspects of the astrological houses (see II.i.100, note) at the time of the infant's birth. Such
practice was common, despite both serious and popular criticism of it.

II.iii.0.1.] Located in some courtyard or open room in the Duchess's
palace.
    dark lantern] a lantern with an arrangement for concealing its light (see
l. 54, below).
    5. *several wards*] various places under guard, apartments.
    have part of it] share in knowledge of it (i.e. the *stratagem*).
    6. *My . . . freeze*] my spying will go cold; I shall not progress in my task as
intelligencer.
    8.] The *owl* was also considered a portent of death.
    14. *mole*] i.e. someone who works in the dark.
    undermine me] seek my downfall by secret and stealthy means.

A noise even now?

Bosola.   From whence?

Antonio.   From the Duchess' lodging.   15

Bosola. Not I. Did you?

Antonio.   I did, or else I dreamed.

Bosola. Let's walk towards it.

Antonio.   No. It may be 'twas
But the rising of the wind.

Bosola.   Very likely.
Methinks 'tis very cold, and yet you sweat:
You look wildly.

Antonio.   I have been setting a figure   20
For the Duchess' jewels.

Bosola.   Ah: and how falls your question?
Do you find it radical?

Antonio.   What's that to you?
'Tis rather to be questioned what design,
When all men were commanded to their lodgings,
Makes you a night-walker.

Bosola.   In sooth, I'll tell you: 25
Now all the court's asleep, I thought the devil
Had least to do here; I came to say my prayers,
And, if it do offend you I do so,
You are a fine courtier.

Antonio. [*Aside*]   This fellow will undo me.
[*To him*] You gave the Duchess apricocks today—   30
Pray heaven they were not poisoned.

Bosola.   Poisoned? A Spanish fig
For the imputation!

Antonio.   Traitors are ever confident

20–1. *setting . . . jewels*] i.e. casting a horoscope to inquire about the stolen goods. So, it was said, thieves could be identified, hiding places revealed, and ultimate recovery or loss predicted.

22. *Do . . . radical?*] i.e. is the timing suitable for making a judgement? *Radical* means fundamental, inherent, fit to be decided.

25. *night-walker*] commonly said of thieves, rogues, etc.

29. *fine*] highly refined, over-zealous (used ironically here).

31. *A Spanish fig*] a contemptuous and phallic gesture of thrusting the thumb between the first and middle finger; also, here, a poisonous fruit, recommended for secret poisoning; with wordplay on *fig* used scornfully for anything of little consequence.

Till they are discovered. There were jewels stol'n too—
In my conceit, none are to be suspected
More than yourself.
Bosola.   You are a false steward.   35
Antonio. Saucy slave! I'll pull thee up by the roots.
Bosola. May be the ruin will crush you to pieces.
    You are an impudent snake indeed, sir.
    Are you scarce warm, and do you show your sting?
Antonio. You libel well, sir.
Bosola.   No, sir; copy it out,   40
    And I will set my hand to 't.
Antonio. [*Aside*]   My nose bleeds.
    One that were superstitious would count
    This ominous, when it merely comes by chance.
    Two letters, that are wrought here for my name,
    Are drowned in blood!   45
    Mere accident. [*To him*] For you, sir, I'll take order:

---

34. *conceit*] opinion.
37. *ruin*] falling down.
38–9.] Q allocates these lines to Antonio, repeating the same prefix at the beginning of l. 40. Obviously this is an error. Possibly the compositor omitted a speech for Bosola which should come between the two he marked for Antonio, but a simpler error would have been for the compositor to antici-pate the prefix at l. 40 and, not realizing his error, set it again at the correct place. (The same compositor certainly confused and/or omitted prefixes elsewhere when setting his part of Q.) The text makes good sense if it is emended by removing the earlier prefix at l. 38. Thus, Bosola counters Antonio's threat of l. 34 and then returns to his attack, repeating 'You are' from his previous denunciation. *Impudent* is a fit epithet for a mere *steward* who has called the Provisor of Horse a 'Saucy slave' and threatened his livelihood ('pull thee up by the roots'); *indeed* marks this denunciation as intensifying an earlier one.
39. *scarce warm*] i.e. only recently having lain in the sun (which here represents his prince's show of special favour).
40. *copy it out*] i.e. the supposed 'libel'. Bosola offers to sign a statement of what he has said and thus be legally liable for slander.
41. *set . . . to 't*] sign it.
44. *wrought*] i.e. embroidered on the handkerchief. Busied with this, Antonio drops the paper on which the horoscope is written.
46. *Mere accident*] i.e. the blood on his name is not another bad portent. Antonio does not know he has dropped incriminating evidence.
    order] appropriate measures.

I'th' morn you shall be safe. [*Aside*] 'Tis that must colour
Her lying-in. [*To him*] Sir, this door you pass not:
I do not hold it fit that you come near
The Duchess' lodgings till you have quit yourself.   50
[*Aside*] *The great are like the base—nay, they are the*
    same—
When they seek shameful ways to avoid shame.   *Exit.*
Bosola. Antonio hereabout did drop a paper.
    Some of your help, false friend.—O, here it is!
    What's here? A child's nativity calculated!   55
    [*Reads*] *The Duchess was delivered of a son, 'tween the hours*
        twelve and one, in the night, Anno Dom. 1504—that's this
        year—*decimo nono Decembris*—that's this night—*taken*
        according to the meridian of Malfi—that's our Duchess:
        happy discovery!—*The lord of the first house, being*   60
        combust in the ascendant, signifies short life; and Mars
        being in a human sign, joined to the tail of the Dragon, in
        the eighth house, doth threaten a violent death. Caetera non
        scrutantur.

---

47. *safe*] safely confined.
'*Tis . . . colour*] it is this subterfuge that must disguise.
50. *quit*] acquitted.
51. *nay . . . same*] a devastating second thought; if this is so, he has not
made a 'noble' marriage and has not bettered himself.
54. *false friend*] i.e. his 'dark lantern'.
56–64.] The horoscope, with its dire prognostication of a violent death, is
astrological gibberish. 'Any professional astrologer would know that if the
child was born between 12 and 1 in the night of 19 December 1504, the sun
must be posited somewhere around the nadir of the chart (i.e. in the third or
fourth houses), and therefore no planet could be "combust in the ascendant"' (A. Borodcicz). However, some astrological know-how was involved in
its composition and is required to make any sense of it: a planet being *combust*
(i.e. burnt up) loses almost all its benign influence; *Mars* is the potentially
destructive God of War; the *human signs* of the zodiac are Gemini, Virgo,
Sagittarius, and Aquarius; the *tail of the Dragon* is that point in the heavens
where the moon crosses the sun's ecliptic in its descent into southern
latitudes—an event that was thought to exert a sinister influence. The son
whose nativity is calculated here is the one child surviving from the marriage
of the Duchess and Antonio; an astrologer would suspect that some benevo-
lent influence, such as Jupiter or Venus, must have been exerted before the
'combustion' and so delayed the disaster. By adding *Caetera non scrutantur*
('the rest is not investigated'), Webster makes it clear that the entire
horoscope has not been investigated.

Why, now 'tis most apparent: this precise fellow   65
Is the Duchess' bawd. I have it to my wish:
This is a parcel of intelligency
Our courtiers were cased up for! It needs must follow
That I must be committed on pretence
Of poisoning her; which I'll endure, and laugh at.   70
If one could find the father now! But that
Time will discover. Old Castruchio
I'th' morning posts to Rome; by him I'll send
A letter that shall make her brothers' galls
O'erflow their livers. This was a thrifty way!   75
Though lust do mask in ne'er so strange disguise,
She's oft found witty, but is never wise.   [*Exit.*]

Scene iv

Enter Cardinal *and* JULIA.

Cardinal. Sit; thou art my best of wishes. Prithee, tell me
          What trick didst thou invent to come to Rome
          Without thy husband.
Julia.   Why, my lord, I told him
          I came to visit an old anchorite
          Here, for devotion.
Cardinal.   Thou art a witty false one—   5
          I mean, to him.
Julia.   You have prevailed with me

---

65. *precise*] scrupulous (sometimes said of Puritans).

fellow] used contemptuously, as if to an inferior.

66. *bawd*] pander, go-between. (Bosola misses the true significance of what he has witnessed.)

67. *parcel*] item, piece.

69. *committed*] imprisoned.

74–5. *her brothers'. . . livers*] i.e. her brothers will be given over entirely to bitterness. The liver was considered to be the seat of passionate feeling.

75. *thrifty*] thriving.

76. mask] (1) hide; (2) take part in gorgeous dances. *Mask* and *masque* were not differentiated in spelling.

II.iv.0.1.] The location is now Rome (as l. 2 makes clear immediately), in a private room belonging to the Cardinal.

5. *devotion*] quibbling on the religious and amatory senses.

witty] an unintentional echo of the previous scene's concluding sentence.

Beyond my strongest thoughts; I would not now
Find you inconstant.
Cardinal.   Do not put thyself
    To such a voluntary torture, which proceeds
    Out of your own guilt.
Julia.   How, my lord?
Cardinal.   You fear   10
    My constancy because you have approved
    Those giddy and wild turnings in yourself.
Julia. Did you e'er find them?
Cardinal.   Sooth, generally for women;
    A man might strive to make glass malleable
    Ere he should make them fixed.
Julia.   So, my lord.   15
Cardinal. We had need go borrow that fantastic glass
    Invented by Galileo the Florentine,
    To view another spacious world i'th' moon
    And look to find a constant woman there.
Julia. This is very well, my lord.
Cardinal.   Why do you weep?   20
    Are tears your justification? The self-same tears
    Will fall into your husband's bosom, lady,
    With a loud protestation, that you love him
    Above the world. Come, I'll love you wisely,
    That's jealously, since I am very certain   25
    You cannot me make cuckold.
Julia.   I'll go home
    To my husband.
Cardinal.   You may thank me, lady,
    I have taken you off your melancholy perch,
    Bore you upon my fist, and showed you game,
    And let you fly at it.—I pray thee, kiss me.—   30

---

11. *approved*] confirmed, made proof of, experienced.

13. *Sooth . . . woman*] Truth to say, I have found such turnings (inconstancies) in all women.

16–17.] Galileo's use of the telescope disproved the earth-centred model of the universe.

19. *a constant woman*] The moon was associated with women in its constant change.

25. *jealously*] (1) ardently, solicitously; (2) suspiciously, watchfully.

28–30. *perch . . . fist . . . game . . . fly*] terms of falconry.

When thou wast with thy husband, thou wast watched
Like a tame elephant.—Still you are to thank me.—
Thou hadst only kisses from him, and high feeding,
But what delight was that? 'Twas just like one
That hath a little fing'ring on the lute,   35
Yet cannot tune it.—Still you are to thank me.
Julia. You told me of a piteous wound i'th' heart,
And a sick liver, when you wooed me first,
And spake like one in physic.
Cardinal.   Who's that?—
Rest firm; for my affection to thee,   40
Lightning moves slow to 't.

Enter Servant.

Servant.   Madam, a gentleman,
That's come post from Malfi, desires to see you.
Cardinal. Let him enter; I'll withdraw.   *Exit.*
Servant.   He says
Your husband, old Castruchio, is come to Rome,

---

31. *watched*] (1) kept awake; (2) kept in sight.

32. *elephant*] The huge and, for Jacobeans, almost fabulous beast was proverbially unmanageable.

32–6. *Still . . . me*] 'I pray thee, kiss me' (l. 30), following soon after 'You may thank me, lady' (l. 27) suggests that the Cardinal was asking for kisses at that point, and now does so again for the second and third times. Julia's next speech (ll. 37–9) is very different in mood from her previous one, as if she has changed under the Cardinal's coaxing, from blunt rejection to more intimacy with a teasing (or, even, nostalgic) reproof. Such prolonged physical contact is very rarely called for in the Jacobean theatre, which used young male actors for all women's roles. *High feeding* = rich repast, luxury.

39. *in physic*] i.e. under the doctor's care.

Who's that?] The Cardinal hears the Servant who is about to enter.

40–1. *Rest . . . to 't*] The Cardinal seems to offer Julia assurances of loving her, but the comparison of love to lightning was usually used to illustrate love's impermanence and destructive ability. *To 't* = in comparison with it.

42. *Malfi*] The word is the first to connect Julia with earlier events in the play; the connection is rapidly made stronger with news that '*old* Castruchio' is her husband (the name has not been heard before, but his coming to Rome in post identifies him with the Old Man seen earlier in the act and in I.i.82–223).

Most pitifully tired with riding post.   [*Exit.*]   45

Enter DELIO.

Julia. [*Aside*] Signior Delio! 'Tis one of my old suitors.
Delio. I was bold to come and see you.
Julia.   Sir, you are welcome.
Delio. Do you lie here?
Julia.   Sure, your own experience
   Will satisfy you no; our Roman prelates
   Do not keep lodging for ladies.
Delio.   Very well.   50
   I have brought you no commendations from your
      husband,
   For I know none by him.
Julia.   I hear he's come to Rome?
Delio. I never knew man and beast, or a horse and a knight,
   So weary of each other; if he had had a good back,
   He would have undertook to have borne his horse,   55
   His breech was so pitifully sore.
Julia.   Your laughter
   Is my pity.
Delio.   Lady, I know not whether
   You want money, but I have brought you some.
                                    [*Offers money.*]
Julia. From my husband?
Delio.   No, from mine own allowance.

45.1 S.D.] Delio's appearance bringing money to purchase Julia's favours
will be a surprise to an audience (although nowhere near so great a shock as
that of seeing the Cardinal with his mistress); hitherto Delio has seemed an
upright and rather earnest foil to Antonio, aware that deceptions were to be
expected at Court but not engaging in any himself. The incident is not
developed in any further scene and leaves little or no mark on what Delio
does subsequently; it adds to the audience's sense of an ever-spreading web
of intrigues and the complexity of characters whose 'insides' are not to be
'understood' easily (see II.i.86–7).
   48. *lie*] reside.
   53. *or*] Q reads 'of', which makes only very awkward sense in the context;
it is preferable to emend, correcting what would be an easy error for *or*. Delio
implies that the real *man* is the *horse* and Castruchio the *beast*.
   54. *had . . . back*] implying that he is impotent as well as weak and a bad
horseman; cf. II.v.73.
   56–7. *Your . . . pity*] You laugh; I find my husband pitiful.

Julia. I must hear the condition, ere I be bound to take it.   60
Delio. Look on 't; 'tis gold. Hath it not a fine colour?
Julia. I have a bird more beautiful.
Delio. Try the sound on 't.
Julia.   A lute-string far exceeds it;
    It hath no smell, like cassia or civet,
    Nor is it physical, though some fond doctors   65
    Persuade us seethe 't in cullises. I'll tell you,
    This is a creature bred by—

                [*Enter* Servant.]

Servant.   Your husband's come,
    Hath delivered a letter to the Duke of Calabria,
    That, to my thinking, hath put him out of his wits.
                                  [*Exit.*]
Julia. Sir, you hear—   70
    Pray, let me know your business and your suit
    As briefly as can be.
Delio.   With good speed. I would wish you,
    At such time as you are non-resident
    With your husband, my mistress.
Julia. Sir, I'll go ask my husband if I shall,   75
    And straight return your answer.   *Exit.*
Delio.   Very fine!
    Is this her wit or honesty that speaks thus?
    I heard one say the Duke was highly moved
    With a letter sent from Malfi. I do fear

---

64. *cassia*] Under the influence of the Bible and of Virgil and Ovid among the poets, this inferior kind of cinnamon was often referred to, in poetic passages, as if it were a plant of great fragrance.

civet] musky perfume derived from the civet cat.

65. *physical*] medicinal.

fond] foolish.

66. *seethe*] boil.

cullises] broths.

67. *This . . . by*] Usurers were criticized for putting money to the unnatural act of begetting more money; Julia is about to say something similar about Delio's offering of gold.

71. *suit*] petition (Julia speaks as if she were a 'great man' giving a hurried audience).

77. *honesty*] (1) truthfulness; (2) chastity.

Antonio is betrayed. How fearfully   80
Shows his ambition now! Unfortunate fortune!
They pass through whirlpools and deep woes do shun,
Who the event weigh ere the action's done.   *Exit.*

Scene v

Enter Cardinal, *and* FERDINAND *with a letter.*

Ferdinand. I have this night digged up a mandrake.
Cardinal.   Say you?
Ferdinand. And I am grown mad with 't.
Cardinal.   What's the prodigy?
Ferdinand. Read there—a sister damned! She's loose i'th'
     hilts,
     Grown a notorious strumpet.
Cardinal.   Speak lower.
Ferdinand.   Lower?
     Rogues do not whisper 't now, but seek to publish 't,   5
     As servants do the bounty of their lords,
     Aloud, and with a covetous, searching eye
     To mark who note them. O, confusion seize her!
     She hath had most cunning bawds to serve her turn,

---

83. event] outcome.

II.v.0.1.] The location is again Rome, but now in one of Ferdinand's private rooms.

1–2. *I . . . with 't*] A *mandrake* (or the poisonous root of the plant mandragora) was formerly used medicinally for its narcotic and emetic properties. When forked this root can look like a caricature of the human form. Many strange beliefs attached to it: it was said to feed on blood (and so often grew by gallows), to utter a shriek when pulled from the ground, and to madden those who heard this sound. Ferdinand's words start what will prove to be a crucial scene in a startling manner, the *mandrake* establishing at once a world of fantasy, vivid sensation, and disfigured, naked bodies. Webster's substitution of *digged* for an expected 'pulled' may give a sense of extreme physical effort.

2. *prodigy*] (1) ill omen; (2) monstrous thing, occasion.

3. *loose i'th' hilts*] (1) unreliable; (2) open to any man. A *hilt* is the handle of a sword or dagger.

7. *covetous*] motivated by hope to be paid for future silence or for information.

8. *confusion*] ruin.

9. *serve her turn*] be useful to her, answer her purpose (in making assignations).

And more secure conveyances for lust
Than towns of garrison for service.   10
Cardinal.   Is 't possible?
Can this be certain?
Ferdinand.   Rhubarb, O, for rhubarb
To purge this choler! Here's the cursèd day
To prompt my memory, and here 't shall stick
Till of her bleeding heart I make a sponge   15
To wipe it out.
Cardinal.   Why do you make yourself
So wild a tempest?
Ferdinand.   Would I could be one,
That I might toss her palace 'bout her ears,
Root up her goodly forests, blast her meads,
And lay her general territory as waste   20
As she hath done her honours.
Cardinal.   Shall our blood,
The royal blood of Aragon and Castile,
Be thus attainted?
Ferdinand.   Apply desperate physic.
We must not now use balsamum, but fire,

---

10. *secure conveyances*] safe means of providing.

11. *service*] supplies. The word was also used of sexual satisfaction.

12–13. *Rhubarb . . . choler*] *Choler*, or 'bile', was considered to be one of the 'four humours' which together formed the 'complexion' or temperament of a person. A well-known medical authority said that it 'stirreth up furious vapors in our spirits, which blind us and cast us headlong to whatsoever may satisfy the desire which we have of revenge'. A common prescription for dealing with an excess of *choler* was *rhubarb*.

13. *Here's*] Ferdinand probably gestures to his head or heart. In this, Webster might have been influenced by Shakespeare's Hamlet who spoke, after he had heard the Ghost's message, of the 'table of my memory' and the 'book and volume of his brain' (*Hamlet*, I.v.97–104). Webster's debt to that play's scenes of Ophelia's madness are very obvious in *W.D.*, V.iv.66–83.

17–21. *Would . . . honours*] The series of nouns directing attention to physical nature, the repeated *her* keeping the Duchess in mind, the strong rhythm which builds towards the end of the sequence of active verbs about physical activity, where they culminate in *lay waste*, will all require an actor to have a strong and vivid sexual imagination that can drive this speech and, hence, his whole performance at this point.

23. *attainted*] The Cardinal seems to use the word legally, as 'held to be stained or corrupted', whereas Ferdinand understands it more physically as 'infected' (see l. 26).

24. *balsamum*] balm, aromatic resin mixed with oils.

The smarting cupping glass, for that's the mean   25
To purge infected blood, such blood as hers.
There is a kind of pity in mine eye;
I'll give it to my handkercher; and, now 'tis here,
I'll bequeath this to her bastard.
Cardinal.   What to do?
Ferdinand. Why, to make soft lint for his mother's wounds,   30
When I have hewed her to pieces.
Cardinal.   Cursed creature!
Unequal Nature, to place women's hearts
So far upon the left side!
Ferdinand.   Foolish men,
That e'er will trust their honour in a bark
Made of so slight, weak bulrush as is woman,   35
Apt every minute to sink it!
Cardinal. Thus ignorance, when it hath purchased honour,
It cannot wield it.
Ferdinand.   Methinks I see her laughing—
Excellent hyena!—Talk to me somewhat, quickly,
Or my imagination will carry me   40
To see her in the shameful act of sin.
Cardinal. With whom?
Ferdinand.   Happily with some strong-thighed bargeman,
Or one o'th' woodyard, that can quoit the sledge

---

25. *cupping glass*] surgical vessel in which a vacuum is created by the application of extreme heat, and then is used to draw off blood.
  mean] means, instrument.
26. *blood*] The Cardinal had used *blood* = 'noble lineage' (l. 21, above), but for Ferdinand it stands for 'passion, sexual appetite', and 'life blood'.
32. *Unequal*] unjust.
32–3. *place . . . side*] Both men and women were sometimes said to be prone to deceit because their hearts were on the left side of their bodies; here the woman's is more so.
37. *purchased*] obtained (often without the idea of paying money or other goods in exchange).
39. *hyena*] animal with a cry like a shrill or mad laugh, very close at hand; mostly a nocturnal wild animal. One kind of female *hyena* was believed to be able to kill a sleeping man by stretching her body upon him; it became a type of treachery, especially in woman.
42. *Happily*] haply, perhaps.
43. *woodyard*]. See II.ii.64, note.
  quoit the sledge] throw the hammer, in public sport; here used with sexual innuendo, as is much else in this speech.

Or toss the bar, or else some lovely squire
That carries coals up to her privy lodgings.　　　　45
Cardinal.　You fly beyond your reason.
Ferdinand.　　　　　　　　　　Go to, mistress!
'Tis not your whore's milk that shall quench my wildfire,
But your whore's blood.
Cardinal.　How idly shows this rage, which carries you,
As men conveyed by witches through the air,　　　　50
On violent whirlwinds! This intemperate noise
Fitly resembles deaf men's shrill discourse,
Who talk aloud, thinking all other men
To have their imperfection.
Ferdinand.　　　　　　　　Have not you
My palsy?
Cardinal.　　　　Yes—I can be angry　　　　55
Without this rupture. There is not in nature
A thing that makes man so deformed, so beastly,
As doth intemperate anger. Chide yourself:
You have divers men who never yet expressed
Their strong desire of rest but by unrest,　　　　60
By vexing of themselves. Come, put yourself
In tune.
Ferdinand.　So. I will only study to seem
The thing I am not.—I could kill her now,
In you, or in myself, for I do think
It is some sin in us heaven doth revenge　　　　65

---

44. *squire*] personal servant, young man.

45. *carries coals*] a common phrase for 'do any dirty work'.

46. *Go to*] an expression of protest or disgust; here also, sarcastically and crudely, 'Go to it.'

47. *wildfire*] (1) inflammable, fast-burning substance used in warfare; (2) uncontrollable passion.

49. *idly*] (1) foolishly; (2) ineffectually.

55. *palsy*] paralysis (here with the involuntary tremors which it sometimes brings).

59. *You . . . men*] One commonly sees men of all sorts.

63. *The . . . not*] presumably, the temperate man that I am not. But these words are ambiguous and may have more devious or more desperate meanings; Ferdinand's next words are, in part, a confession of guilt for a *sin* which he does not name. But this reaction is only momentary, and he proceeds to exercise his fervid imagination in thinking of sadistically cruel revenges.

By her.

Cardinal.   Are you stark mad?

Ferdinand.   I would have their bodies
Burnt in a coal-pit, with the ventage stopped,
That their cursed smoke might not ascend to heaven;
Or dip the sheets they lie in in pitch or sulphur,
Wrap them in 't, and then light them like a match;   70
Or else to boil their bastard to a cullis,
And give 't his lecherous father, to renew
The sin of his back.

Cardinal.   I'll leave you.

Ferdinand.   Nay, I have done.
I am confident, had I been damned in hell
And should have heard of this, it would have put me   75
Into a cold sweat.—In, in; I'll go sleep.—
Till I know who leaps my sister, I'll not stir:
That known, I'll find scorpions to string my whips,
And fix her in a general eclipse.   *Exeunt.*

---

66. *their bodies*] the bodies of the Duchess and her lover.

67. *coal-pit*] pit for making charcoal.

ventage] vent-hole left for smoke to rise out.

71. *cullis*] broth.

73. *of his back*] i.e. of his hot flesh.

76. *I'll go sleep*] After great expenditure of energy, Ferdinand is suddenly exhausted; or, possibly, he is now able to 'seem / The thing [he is] not' (ll. 62–3). At the beginning of the next act, Ferdinand's very quietness strikes Antonio as the most dangerous thing about him (III.i.19–24). Webster has been taken to task for allowing Ferdinand to be inactive for two or three years following the discovery of his sister's child, but throughout the play he is portrayed as alternately passionate and paralysed, active and withdrawn, verbal and silent. See also the Introduction on Webster's techniques for creating stage-characters.

78. *scorpions . . . whips*] a Biblical idea; see 1 Kings, 12.11—'My father hath chastised you with whips, but I will chastise you with scorpions'—where 'scorpions' was thought to mean knotted or barbed scourges.

79. *general*] total.

Act III

Scene i

Enter ANTONIO *and* DELIO.

Antonio. Our noble friend, my most belovèd Delio!
　　O, you have been a stranger long at court;
　　Came you along with the Lord Ferdinand?
Delio. I did, sir; and how fares your noble Duchess?
Antonio. Right fortunately well. She's an excellent　　　5
　　Feeder of pedigrees; since you last saw her,
　　She hath had two children more, a son and daughter.
Delio. Methinks 'twas yesterday. Let me but wink,
　　And not behold your face, which to mine eye
　　Is somewhat leaner, verily I should dream　　　10
　　It were within this half hour.
Antonio. You have not been in law, friend Delio,
　　Nor in prison, nor a suitor at the court,
　　Nor begged the reversion of some great man's place,
　　Nor troubled with an old wife, which doth make　　　15
　　Your time so insensibly hasten.
Delio. 　　　　　　　　　Pray, sir, tell me,
　　Hath not this news arrived yet to the ear
　　Of the Lord Cardinal?
Antonio. 　　　　　　　I fear it hath:

III.i.0.1.] Located, once more, at Malfi, in an ante-chamber of the palace.
　1. *noble*] with some irony for the audience, which has witnessed Delio's part in II.iv.
　2. *long*] at least two years, sufficient time for the Duchess to give birth to two more children.
　5–7.] Antonio is sufficiently confident and/or unfeeling to joke about the Duchess's childbearing and the growing dangers of their secret marriage. Delio catches his boastful and playful tone in ll. 8–11.
　8. *wink*] close my eyes.
　16. *insensibly*] (1) imperceptibly; (2) foolishly.
　18. *Lord Cardinal*] Because he has direct experience of the Cardinal's duplicity, Delio may think that the Cardinal would hear before Ferdinand.

The Lord Ferdinand, that's newly come to court,
Doth bear himself right dangerously.

Delio.   Pray, why?   20

Antonio. He is so quiet that he seems to sleep
The tempest out, as dormice do in winter:
Those houses that are haunted are most still,
Till the devil be up.

Delio.   What say the common people?

Antonio. The common rabble do directly say   25
She is a strumpet.

Delio.   And your graver heads,
Which would be politic, what censure they?

Antonio. They do observe I grow to infinite purchase
The left-hand way, and all suppose the Duchess
Would amend it, if she could; for, say they,   30
Great princes, though they grudge their officers
Should have such large and unconfinèd means
To get wealth under them, will not complain
Lest thereby they should make them odious
Unto the people—for other obligation   35
Of love, or marriage, between her and me,
They never dream of.

Enter FERDINAND *and* Duchess.

Delio.   The Lord Ferdinand
Is going to bed.

Ferdinand.   I'll instantly to bed,
For I am weary.—I am to bespeak
A husband for you.

Duchess.   For me, sir! Pray, who is 't?   40

Ferdinand. The great Count Malateste.

Duchess.   Fie upon him,

---

22. *dormice*] See I.i.282, and note. 'To sleep like a dormouse' was
proverbial.

23. *still*] quiet.

25. *directly*] plainly, simply.

27. *censure*] judge.

28. *purchase*] acquisitions, wealth.

34–5. *make . . . people*] i.e. make them hated by the people by drawing
attention to their extortions.

A count? He's a mere stick of sugar candy;
You may look quite thorough him. When I choose
A husband, I will marry for your honour.
Ferdinand. You shall do well in 't.—How is 't, worthy
　　Antonio?   45
Duchess. But sir, I am to have private conference with you
　　About a scandalous report is spread
　　Touching mine honour.
Ferdinand.　　　　　　Let me be ever deaf to 't:
　　One of Pasquil's paper bullets, court calumny,
　　A pestilent air which princes' palaces   50
　　Are seldom purged of. Yet, say that it were true—
　　I pour it in your bosom—my fixed love
　　Would strongly excuse, extenuate, nay, deny
　　Faults, were they apparent in you. Go, be safe
　　In your own innocency.
Duchess. [*Aside*]　　　　O blessed comfort!   55
　　This deadly air is purged.
　　　　　　　　　　　Exeunt [*all except* FERDINAND].
Ferdinand.　　　　　　　　Her guilt treads on
　　Hot-burning coulters.

　　　　　　　　　　Enter BOSOLA.

　　　　　　　　　　Now, Bosola,

---

42. *sugar candy*] In *The Devil's Law Case*, Webster uses the idea again: 'You are a fool, a precious one—you are a mere stick of sugar candy; a man may look quite through you' (II.i.153–5).

45. *How is 't?*] how are you? Supposing him to be his sister's pander, Ferdinand tries to make Antonio betray his complicity; she immediately diverts attention.

49. *Pasquil's paper bullets*] lampoons. Pasquil was the name given to a mutilated statue discovered in Rome in 1501 and set up near Piazza Navona; it became a custom to fix satirical and topical verses on this statue on St Mark's day. Original 'pasquinades' in Latin were published in 1544 and the form imitated in other countries; the vogue was greatest in Italy in 1585–90.

52. *I . . . bosom*] I confide in you. A common phrase, but Webster uses it for special intimacies, as in Bracciano's first appeal to Vittoria in *W.D.*, I.ii.206.

56–7.] Ordeal by walking barefoot over red-hot *coulters*, or ploughshares, was known in ancient English law as a means of vindicating assertions of chastity.

How thrives our intelligence?

Bosola.   Sir, uncertainly:
'Tis rumoured she hath had three bastards, but
By whom, we may go read i'th' stars.

Ferdinand.   Why, some   60
Hold opinion all things are written there.

Bosola. Yes, if we could find spectacles to read them.
I do suspect there hath been some sorcery
Used on the Duchess.

Ferdinand.   Sorcery! To what purpose?

Bosola. To make her dote on some desertless fellow   65
She shames to acknowledge.

Ferdinand.   Can your faith give way
To think there's pow'r in potions, or in charms,
To make us love, whether we will or no?

Bosola. Most certainly.

Ferdinand. Away! These are mere gulleries, horrid things   70
Invented by some cheating mountebanks
To abuse us. Do you think that herbs or charms
Can force the will? Some trials have been made
In this foolish practice, but the ingredients
Were lenitive poisons, such as are of force   75
To make the patient mad; and straight the witch
Swears, by equivocation, they are in love.
The witchcraft lies in her rank blood: this night
I will force confession from her. You told me
You had got, within these two days, a false key   80
Into her bed-chamber.

Bosola.   I have.

Ferdinand.   As I would wish.

66–79. *Can . . . her*] The great detail and energetic phrasing of this digression show how readily Ferdinand is drawn to question the sources of sexual longing.

70. *gulleries*] tricks.

71. *mountebanks*] charlatans, itinerant quacks who sold cures etc. in public places at fairs and on market days.

73. *will*] (1) sexual desire, appetite; (2) wish, intention, power of choice.

75. *lenitive*] soothing (so that the poison works secretly).

78. *witchcraft*] See I.i.259, note.

Bosola. What do you intend to do?
Ferdinand.   Can you guess?
Bosola.   No.
Ferdinand. Do not ask, then:

    He that can compass me, and know my drifts,
    May say he hath put a girdle 'bout the world   85
    And sounded all her quicksands.

Bosola.   I do not
    Think so.
Ferdinand.   What do you think then, pray?
Bosola.   That you
    Are your own chronicle too much, and grossly
    Flatter yourself.
Ferdinand.   Give me thy hand; I thank thee.
    I never gave pension but to flatterers,   90
    Till I entertained thee. Farewell.
    That friend a great man's ruin strongly checks
    Who rails into his belief all his defects.   *Exeunt.*

Scene ii

        Enter Duchess, ANTONIO *and* CARIOLA.

Duchess. Bring me the casket hither, and the glass.—
    You get no lodging here tonight, my lord.
Antonio. Indeed, I must persuade one.
Duchess.   Very good:

---

    82. *Can you guess?*] The metre suggests a stress on *you*.

    84. *compass*] comprehend, reach all round. A further sense of 'use a compass, navigate' seems valid, in view of 'drifts' and the following two lines.

    85. *put . . . world*] a proverbial phrase, after Drake's circumnavigation of the world, commonly used of daring actions and great ambitions.

    87-8. *you . . . much*] According to Francisco, in *W.D.*, ''Tis a ridiculous thing for a man to be his own chronicle' (V.i.100–1).

    92–3.] One who unsparingly criticizes a great man's defects shows true friendship in preventing that great man's undoing.

    III.ii.0.1.] The location is the Duchess's bedroom at Malfi.

    1.] The Duchess is preparing for bed; the *casket* is for the jewels she takes off, the mirror so that she may take down and brush her hair (see l. 53, below). While she is absorbed in this business, Cariola and Antonio talk among themselves (ll. 11–20).

                    I hope in time 'twill grow into a custom
                    That noblemen shall come with cap and knee   5
                    To purchase a night's lodging of their wives.
Antonio. I must lie here.
Duchess.   Must? You are a lord of mis-rule.
Antonio. Indeed, my rule is only in the night.
Duchess. To what use will you put me?
Antonio.   We'll sleep together.
Duchess. Alas, what pleasure can two lovers find in sleep?   10
Cariola. My lord, I lie with her often, and I know
                    She'll much disquiet you—
Antonio.   See, you are complained of.
Cariola. For she's the sprawling'st bedfellow.
Antonio. I shall like her the better for that.
Cariola. Sir, shall I ask you a question?   15
Antonio. I pray thee, Cariola.
Cariola. Wherefore still when you lie with my lady
                    Do you rise so early?
Antonio.   Labouring men
                    Count the clock oft'nest, Cariola,
                    Are glad when their task's ended.
Duchess.   I'll stop your mouth.   20
                                              [*Kisses him.*]
Antonio. Nay, that's but one. Venus had two soft doves
                    To draw her chariot; I must have another.   [*Kisses her.*]
                    When wilt thou marry, Cariola?
Cariola.   Never, my lord.
Antonio. O, fie upon this single life! Forgo it!
                    We read how Daphne, for her peevish flight,   25

---

    5. *with . . . knee*] an informal version of 'with cap in hand and bended
knee'.

    7. *lord of mis-rule*] one chosen to preside over feasts and revels at Court,
universities, great houses, etc.; he would be very young or of low status, and
so the custom overturned the usual exercise of power. Q's hyphen is retained
here to point the quibble.

    17. *still*] always.

    25–6. *Daphne . . . bay tree*] Pursued by an enamoured Apollo, Daphne
asked the gods for help and was saved by being metamorphosed into a laurel
tree, which Apollo thereafter loved above all trees. *Bay tree* is the English
name for (L.) *Laurus nobilis.*

    peevish] (1) willful, obstinate; (2) silly.

Became a fruitless bay tree, Syrinx turned
To the pale empty reed, Anaxarete
Was frozen into marble; whereas those
Which married, or proved kind unto their friends,
Were by a gracious influence transshaped   30
Into the olive, pomegranate, mulberry;
Became flow'rs, precious stones, or eminent stars.
Cariola. This is a vain poetry. But I pray you, tell me,
    If there were proposed me wisdom, riches, and beauty,
    In three several young men, which should I choose?   35
Antonio. 'Tis a hard question. This was Paris' case,
    And he was blind in 't, and there was great cause;
    For how was 't possible he could judge right,
    Having three amorous goddesses in view,
    And they stark naked? 'Twas a motion   40
    Were able to benight the apprehension
    Of the severest counsellor of Europe.
    Now I look on both your faces so well formed,
    It puts me in mind of a question I would ask.

---

flight] Q read 'slight', which is an easy error for the compositor to make. However, *flight* is what Daphne is renowned for, and 'slight' hardly conveys the effect of her action in running away from Apollo. It seems redundant after 'peevish'.

26–7. *Syrinx . . . reed*] Pursued by an enamoured Pan, Syrinx threw herself into a river; there she was metamorphosed into a *reed*, from which Pan made a pipe on which he played.

27–8. *Anaxarete . . . marble*] Iphis hanged himself at *Anaxarete*'s door; Venus metamorphosed her to stone for being unaffected as Iphis' body was taken to its grave.

29. *friends*] often used of lovers of either sex.

30–1. *transshaped . . . mulberry*] Neither *olive* nor *pomegranate* are associated with any well-known metamorphosis. The *mulberry*'s fruit turned red from the blood of Pyramus, who slew himself because he thought Thisbe, his love, was dead. (Webster found all three fruits together in this context in the passage from George Whetstone's *Heptameron of Civil Discourses* (1582), the source of this entire speech.)

33. *vain*] worthless, foolish.

34. *proposed me*] put before me.

35. *several*] different.

36. *Paris' case*] Paris was called upon to judge between Athene (wisdom), Hera (riches), and Aphrodite (beauty).

40. *motion*] (1) proposal; (2) incitement; (3) spectacle, show.

41. *Were*] that would have been.

Cariola. What is 't?

Antonio.   I do wonder why hard-favoured ladies,   45
        For the most part, keep worse-favoured waiting-women
        To attend them, and cannot endure fair ones.

Duchess. O, that's soon answered.
        Did you ever in your life know an ill painter
        Desire to have his dwelling next door to the shop   50
        Of an excellent picture-maker? 'Twould disgrace
        His face-making, and undo him.—I prithee,
        When were we so merry?—My hair tangles.

Antonio. [*Aside to Cariola*] Pray thee, Cariola, let's steal forth
            the room
        And let her talk to herself; I have divers times   55
        Served her the like, when she hath chafed extremely:
        I love to see her angry. Softly, Cariola.

                                    Exit with CARIOLA.

Duchess. Doth not the colour of my hair 'gin to change?
        When I wax grey, I shall have all the court
        Powder their hair with arras, to be like me.—   60
        You have cause to love me; I entered you into my heart
        Before you would vouchsafe to call for the keys.

                    Enter FERDINAND [*behind*].

        We shall one day have my brothers take you napping:
        Methinks his presence, being now in court,
        Should make you keep your own bed.—But, you'll say,   65
        Love mixed with fear is sweetest.—I'll assure you
        You shall get no more children till my brothers
        Consent to be your gossips.—Have you lost your
            tongue?   [*Turns and sees Ferdinand.*]
        'Tis welcome;
        For know, whether I am doomed to live or die,   70
        I can do both like a prince.

                            Ferdinand gives her a poniard.

Ferdinand.   Die then, quickly!

---

    60. *arras*] powder of orris-root.
    68. *gossips*] godfathers (to your children).
    68.1.] Alternatively, the Duchess sees Ferdinand in the glass (see l. 1) in
which she is looking to attend to her hair.
    71 S.D. *poniard*] presumably their father's (cf. I.i.331). It was presented
with a strange formality before, and is so now (see ll. 149–54, below).

Virtue, where art thou hid? What hideous thing
Is it that doth eclipse thee?
Duchess.   Pray sir, hear me!
Ferdinand. Or is it true, thou art but a bare name,
And no essential thing?
Duchess.   Sir—
Ferdinand.   Do not speak.
Duchess.   No, sir: 75
I will plant my soul in mine ears to hear you.
Ferdinand. O most imperfect light of human reason,
That mak'st us so unhappy, to foresee
What we can least prevent!—Pursue thy wishes,
And glory in them; there's in shame no comfort   80
But to be past all bounds and sense of shame.
Duchess. I pray sir, hear me: I am married.
Ferdinand.   So.
Duchess. Happily, not to your liking; but for that,
Alas, your shears do come untimely now
To clip the bird's wings that's already flown!   85
Will you see my husband?
Ferdinand.   Yes, if I could change
Eyes with a basilisk.
Duchess.   Sure, you came hither
By his confederacy.
Ferdinand.   The howling of a wolf
Is music to thee, screech-owl. Prithee, peace!—
Whate'er thou art, that hast enjoyed my sister—   90
For I am sure thou hear'st me—for thine own sake
Let me not know thee. I came hither prepared
To work thy discovery, yet am now persuaded
It would beget such violent effects
As would damn us both. I would not for ten millions   95

---

73. *eclipse*] with a possible pun on *clips*, embraces.

75. *essential*] real.

79–81. *Pursue . . . shame*] i.e. Go ahead and revel in your shame; shame gives no other comfort than to be shameless.

83. *Happily*] haply, perhaps.

87. *basilisk*] a fabulous reptile that was able to strike a person dead by its look.

89. *to thee*] compared to thee.

90. *thou*] Ferdinand addresses the Duchess's absent lover.

I had beheld thee; therefore use all means
I never may have knowledge of thy name;
Enjoy thy lust still, and a wretched life,
On that condition.—And for thee, vile woman,
If thou do wish thy lecher may grow old   100
In thy embracements, I would have thee build
Such a room for him as our anchorites
To holier use inhabit. Let not the sun
Shine on him till he's dead. Let dogs and monkeys
Only converse with him, and such dumb things   105
To whom nature denies use to sound his name.
Do not keep a paraquito, lest she learn it.
If thou do love him, cut out thine own tongue
Lest it bewray him.
Duchess.   Why might not I marry?
I have not gone about, in this, to create   110
Any new world, or custom.
Ferdinand.   Thou art undone;
And thou hast ta'en that massy sheet of lead
That hid thy husband's bones, and folded it
About my heart.
Duchess.   Mine bleeds for 't.
Ferdinand.   Thine? Thy heart?
What should I name 't, unless a hollow bullet   115
Filled with unquenchable wildfire?
Duchess.   You are, in this,
Too strict; and, were you not my princely brother,
I would say too wilful. My reputation
Is safe.
Ferdinand. Dost thou know what reputation is?
I'll tell thee—to small purpose, since th' instruction   120
Comes now too late.

---

102. *anchorites*] religious recluses, hermits.

106. *use*] ability.

107. *paraquito*] small parrot.

109. *bewray*] reveal, make known.

115. *bullet*] missile. Explosive shells were introduced in place of solid cannon-balls during the sixteenth century.

116. *wildfire*] inflammable material; but see II.v.47 and note.

118. *wilful*] passionate (see also III.i.73, and note). It is used in the same sense in *W.D.*, II.i.41.

Upon a time, Reputation, Love, and Death
Would travel o'er the world; and it was concluded
That they should part, and take three several ways.
Death told them they should find him in great battles,   125
Or cities plagued with plagues. Love gives them counsel
To inquire for him 'mongst unambitious shepherds,
Where dowries were not talked of, and sometimes
'Mongst quiet kindred that had nothing left
By their dead parents. 'Stay', quoth Reputation,   130
'Do not forsake me; for it is my nature
If once I part from any man I meet
I am never found again.' And so, for you:
You have shook hands with Reputation,
And made him invisible. So, fare you well.   135 .
I will never see you more.
Duchess. Why should only I,
Of all the other princes of the world,
Be cased up, like a holy relic? I have youth,
And a little beauty.
Ferdinand.   So you have some virgins   140
That are witches.—I will never see thee more.   *Exit.*

Enter ANTONIO *with a pistol*[, *and* CARIOLA].

Duchess. You saw this apparition?
Antonio.   Yes; we are
Betrayed. How came he hither?—I should turn
This to thee, for that.
Cariola.   Pray, sir, do; and when
That you have cleft my heart, you shall read there   145
Mine innocence.
Duchess.   That gallery gave him entrance.

---

122. *Upon*] once upon.

124. *several*] different.

134. *shook hands with*] i.e. bade farewell to.

140–1. *So . . . witches*] See I.i.259, and note.

141. *I . . . more*] preparing for IV.i (see, especially, ll. 23–8). The repetition from l. 136 adds to the force of this strong exit-line; IV.i.23 requires it to be both 'solemn' and 'rash' in performance.

142. *apparition*] Meanings ranged from 'spectre, illusion' to 'phenomenon, appearance'.

143–4. *turn . . . that*] i.e. point this pistol at you, Cariola, for betraying us.

Antonio. I would this terrible thing would come again,
      That, standing on my guard, I might relate
      My warrantable love.   *She shows the poniard.*
                          Ha! What means this?
Duchess. He left this with me.
Antonio.   And it seems did wish   150
      You would use it on yourself?
Duchess.   His action seemed
      To intend so much.
Antonio.   This hath a handle to 't
      As well as a point—turn it towards him,
      And so fasten the keen edge in his rank gall.
                                    [*Knocking within.*]
      How now! Who knocks? More earthquakes?
Duchess.   I stand   155
      As if a mine, beneath my feet, were ready
      To be blown up.
Cariola.   'Tis Bosola.
Duchess.   Away!
      O misery! Methinks unjust actions
      Should wear these masks and curtains, and not we.—
      You must instantly part hence; I have fashioned it
          already.   *Exit* ANTONIO.   160

                    Enter BOSOLA.

Bosola. The Duke your brother is ta'en up in a whirlwind,
      Hath took horse, and 's rid post to Rome.
Duchess.   So late?
Bosola. He told me, as he mounted into th' saddle,
      You were undone.
Duchess.   Indeed, I am very near it.
Bosola. What's the matter?   165
Duchess. Antonio, the master of our household,
      Hath dealt so falsely with me, in 's accounts:
      My brother stood engaged with me for money

---

158. *unjust*] faithless, dishonest.
168–70.] i.e. Ferdinand was security (*stood engaged*) for money that I had
borrowed (*ta'en up*), and Antonio, by some breach of contract (as failure to
pay due interest), is responsible for (*lets*) Ferdinand becoming liable for the
sum borrowed (*bonds be forfeit*).

  Ta'en up of certain Neapolitan Jews,
  And Antonio lets the bonds be forfeit.   170
Bosola. Strange!—[*Aside*] This is cunning.
Duchess.   And hereupon
  My brother's bills at Naples are protested
  Against.—Call up our officers.
Bosola.   I shall.   *Exit.*

     [*Enter* ANTONIO.]

Duchess. The place that you must fly to is Ancona;
  Hire a house there. I'll send after you   175
  My treasure and my jewels.—Our weak safety
  Runs upon enginous wheels; short syllables
  Must stand for periods. I must now accuse you
  Of such a feignèd crime as Tasso calls
  Magnanima menzogna: a noble lie,   180
  'Cause it must shield our honours.—Hark! They are
   coming.

    Enter [BOSOLA *and*] Officers.

Antonio. Will your grace hear me?
Duchess. I have got well by you! You have yielded me
  A million of loss; I am like to inherit
  The people's curses for your stewardship. 185
  You had the trick in audit-time to be sick,
  Till I had signed your *quietus*, and that cured you

172–3. *My . . . Against*] i.e. it has been formally declared (*protested*) that Ferdinand's promisory notes (*bills*) are not acceptable.

176–7. *Our . . . wheels*] 'The world runs on wheels' was a proverb, implying haste and impermanence. *Enginous* = like an engine or, more usually, 'crafty, cunning, ingenious, intricate'.

179–80. *feignèd . . .* menzogna] from Tasso's *Jerusalem Delivered* (1576–93), II.22, where Soprina takes the blame for rescuing a statue of the Virgin from a mosque in order to prevent wholesale persecution of Christians.

182.] Antonio begins the serious play-acting of a scene designed to quiet suspicions.

183–93.] By repeated wordplay the Duchess sends secret messages to Antonio (comparable to those in II.i.122ff.): *got well . . . yielded me . . .* quietus (echoing I.i.464) . . . *cured . . . be an example . . . hold my favour . . . h'as done that.* 'I pray, *let* him' (l. 190) can mean both 'let him go' and 'let him remain'.

184. *like*] likely.

Without help of a doctor.—Gentlemen,
I would have this man be an example to you all;
So shall you hold my favour. I pray, let him, 190
For h'as done that, alas, you would not think of,
And, because I intend to be rid of him,
I mean not to publish.—Use your fortune elsewhere.
Antonio. I am strongly armed to brook my overthrow,
As commonly men bear with a hard year. 195
I will not blame the cause on 't, but do think
The necessity of my malevolent star
Procures this, not her humour. O the inconstant
And rotten ground of service!—You may see:
'Tis ev'n like him that in a winter night 200
Takes a long slumber o'er a dying fire
As loth to part from 't, yet parts thence as cold
As when he first sat down.
Duchess.   We do confiscate,
Towards the satisfying of your accounts,
All that you have. 205
Antonio. I am all yours; and 'tis very fit
All mine should be so.
Duchess.   So, sir; you have your pass.
Antonio. You may see, gentlemen, what 'tis to serve
A prince with body and soul.   *Exit.*
Bosola. Here's an example for extortion: what moisture is 210
drawn out of the sea, when foul weather comes, pours
down and runs into the sea again.
Duchess. I would know what are your opinions of this
Antonio.

---

193. *Use your fortune*] The Duchess has already secretly decided to follow
Antonio into exile. *Use* was a common word for sexual intercourse. For
fortune in this context, see I.i.495.

194. *brook*] endure.

199. *You*] all you who witness this dismissal.

206–9.] While seeming to submit to the accusation of theft, Antonio
speaks secretly of their marriage; the Duchess, very briefly, acknowledges this
as they are about to part.

210–12.] i.e. Antonio's wealth, which he has extorted while in the
service of the Duchess, has been confiscated and so justly returns to the
Duchess.

Second Officer. He could not abide to see a pig's head gaping.   215
    I thought your grace would find him a Jew.
Third Officer. I would you had been his officer, for your own
    sake.
Fourth Officer. You would have had more money.
First Officer. He stopped his ears with black wool, and to   220
    those came to him for money said he was thick of hearing.
Second Officer. Some said he was an hermaphrodite, for he
    could not abide a woman.
Fourth Officer. How scurvy proud he would look when the
    treasury was full! Well, let him go.   225
First Officer. Yes, and the chippings of the buttery fly after
    him, to scour his gold chain.
Duchess. Leave us.   *Exeunt* Officers.
    What do you think of these?
Bosola. That these are rogues, that in 's prosperity,   230
    But to have waited on his fortune, could have wished
    His dirty stirrup riveted through their noses,
    And followed after's mule, like a bear in a ring;
    Would have prostituted their daughters to his lust;
    Made their first-born intelligencers; thought none happy   235
    But such as were born under his blessed planet,
    And wore his livery: and do these lice drop off now?
    Well, never look to have the like again.
    He hath left a sort of flatt'ring rogues behind him;
    Their doom must follow. Princes pay flatterers   240
    In their own money: flatterers dissemble their vices,
    And they dissemble their lies: that's justice.—

215–16.] a conflation of two proverbs: 'Some cannot abide to see a pig's
head gaping' (i.e. a roasted pig with an apple in its mouth) and 'Invite not a
Jew either to pig or pork' (because this food was forbidden by their religion).

220. *black wool*] recommended as a cure to those who were deaf.

224. *scurvy*] shabbily, discourteously.

226. *the chippings*] let the crumbs, droppings.

227. *gold chain*] worn as sign of his office as steward.

233. *in a ring*] i.e. led by a ring through its nose.

237. *lice*] a common image for flatterers; lice were supposed to leave a
body as soon as the blood failed.

239. *sort*] set, gang.

242. *they*] princes, who repay the flatterers for their dissimulation by
deceiving them in turn. (But, Bosola suggests, Antonio was not like that.)

Alas, poor gentleman!
Duchess. Poor? He hath amply filled his coffers.
Bosola.   Sure
 He was too honest. Pluto, the god of riches,   245
 When he's sent by Jupiter to any man
 He goes limping, to signify that wealth
 That comes on God's name comes slowly; but when he's
 sent on the devil's errand, he rides post and comes in by
 scuttles.   250
 Let me show you what a most unvalued jewel
 You have, in a wanton humour, thrown away,
 To bless the man shall find him. He was an excellent
 Courtier, and most faithful; a soldier that thought it
 As beastly to know his own value too little   255
 As devilish to acknowledge it too much.
 Both his virtue and form deserved a far better fortune.
 His discourse rather delighted to judge itself than show
  itself.
 His breast was filled with all perfection,
 And yet it seemed a private whisp'ring-room,   260
 It made so little noise of 't.
Duchess.   But he was basely descended.
Bosola. Will you make yourself a mercenary herald,
 Rather to examine men's pedigrees than virtues?
 You shall want him;
 For know an honest statesman to a prince   265
 Is like a cedar, planted by a spring;
 The spring bathes the tree's root, the grateful tree

---

245. *Pluto . . . riches*] The *god of riches* was properly called Plutus, but he was sometimes given the name of the god of the underworld; the original forms of both names are related, but when *Pluto* is used for the god of wealth it may well be as a mark of the 'devil', since gold comes from underground.
 248. *on*] in.
 249. *post*] as quickly as possible.
 249–50. *comes . . . scuttles*] obscure in meaning: either 'enters with quick, short steps' or 'delivers his goods in large baskets' (as used for vegetables, etc.).
 251. *unvalued*] (1) invaluable; (2) not regarded as of value.
 253. *shall*] who shall.
 258. *discourse*] wit, faculty of reasoning.
 265. *know*] i.e. take note that.

Rewards it with his shadow: you have not done so.
I would sooner swim to the Bermudas on
Two politicians' rotten bladders, tied   270
Together with an intelligencer's heartstring,
Than depend on so changeable a prince's favour.
Fare thee well, Antonio; since the malice of the world
Would needs down with thee, it cannot be said yet
That any ill happened unto thee,   275
Considering thy fall was accompanied with virtue.
Duchess. O, you render me excellent music.
Bosola.   Say you?
Duchess. This good one that you speak of is my husband.
Bosola. Do I not dream? Can this ambitious age
Have so much goodness in 't as to prefer   280
A man merely for worth, without these shadows
Of wealth and painted honours? Possible?
Duchess. I have had three children by him.
Bosola.   Fortunate lady!
For you have made your private nuptial bed
The humble and fair seminary of peace.   285
No question but many an unbeneficed scholar
Shall pray for you for this deed, and rejoice
That some preferment in the world can yet
Arise from merit. The virgins of your land

---

269. *Bermudas*] Especially after a wreck in 1609, these 'still-vexed' islands
were notorious for strange noises and creatures, as well as for storms and
dangers.

on] i.e. supported by.

270. *bladders*] This fantasy is a grotesque satire: the air, blown into the
bladders, would be leaking out because they are (like the *politicians* or in-
triguers) *rotten*.

271. *intelligencer's*] with secret irony, since Bosola is himself a paid
intelligencer, as he is quick to remember at l. 331, below.

274. *down with thee*] overthrow you.

278.] The very simple wording is both effective and affective, especially in
contrast with the heightened and even laboured style of Bosola's preceding
speech (and much else in this scene).

280. *prefer*] (1) give advancement to; (2) choose, hold in esteem.

281. *without . . . shadows*] i.e. without the substance (of true moral *worth*).

282. *painted*] false, specious.

285. *seminary*] seed bed, breeding-place, nursery.

287. *pray for*] say prayers for.

That have no dowries shall hope your example   290
Will raise them to rich husbands. Should you want
Soldiers, 'twould make the very Turks and Moors
Turn Christians, and serve you for this act.
Last, the neglected poets of your time,
In honour of this trophy of a man,   295
Raised by that curious engine, your white hand,
Shall thank you in your grave for 't, and make that
More reverend than all the cabinets
Of living princes. For Antonio,
His fame shall likewise flow from many a pen,   300
When heralds shall want coats to sell to men.
Duchess. As I taste comfort in this friendly speech,
    So would I find concealment.
Bosola.   O, the secret of my prince,
    Which I will wear on th' inside of my heart!   305
Duchess. You shall take charge of all my coin and jewels,
    And follow him, for he retires himself
    To Ancona.
Bosola.   So.
Duchess.   Whither, within few days,
    I mean to follow thee.
Bosola.   Let me think:
    I would wish your grace to feign a pilgrimage   310

---

296. *curious*] skilfully, beautifully made, exquisite.

engine] instrument, device.

297. *Shall . . . for 't*] will write commemorative poems in your honour for
it.

298. *reverend*] venerated.

cabinets] private rooms (which, in contrast to a *grave*, contain *living* and
most powerful people).

299. *For*] as for.

301.] The granting of arms by the Heralds' College was subject to abuse,
and in 1609 a royal commission was set up to inquire into the sale of spurious
pedigrees.

310–15. *I . . . you*] Bosola could be trying to achieve two aims by offering
to help the Duchess escape: (1) to gain her confidence; (2) to dishonour her
still more by encouraging her to 'jest with religion' and desert her Duchy. In
W.D., Francisco acted against Bracciano by prompting him to 'marry a
whore' (IV.iii.52–6).

To Our Lady of Loretto, scarce seven leagues
From fair Ancona; so may you depart
Your country with more honour, and your flight
Will seem a princely progress, retaining
Your usual train about you.

Duchess.   Sir, your direction   315
Shall lead me by the hand.

Cariola.   In my opinion,
She were better progress to the baths
At Lucca, or go visit the Spa
In Germany, for, if you will believe me,
I do not like this jesting with religion,   320
This feignèd pilgrimage.

Duchess. Thou art a superstitious fool!
Prepare us instantly for our departure.—
Past sorrows, let us moderately lament them;
For those to come, seek wisely to prevent them.   325

                              Exit [*with* CARIOLA].

Bosola. A politician is the devil's quilted anvil:
He fashions all sins on him, and the blows
Are never heard; he may work in a lady's chamber,
As here for proof. What rests but I reveal
All to my lord? O, this base quality   330
Of intelligencer! Why, every quality i'th' world
Prefers but gain or commendation:
Now, for this act I am certain to be raised,
And men that paint weeds to the life are praised.   *Exit.*

---

314. *progress*] state journey.

315. *train*] retinue.

318. *Spa*] The town is some sixteen miles south of Liège in Belgium (often included in the more general term of *Germany*).

320–1.] Cariola voices what many of Webster's contemporaries would consider a serious objection; see III.iii.60–5.

324.] Let us moderately lament past sorrows.

329. *rests*] remains.

330. *quality*] profession.

332. *Prefers*] assists in bringing about, promotes.
but] only.

Scene iii

  Enter Cardinal *with* MALATESTE, FERDINAND *with* DELIO
     and SILVIO, *and* PESCARA.
Cardinal. Must we turn soldier, then?
Malateste.   The Emperor,
  Hearing your worth that way ere you attained
  This reverend garment, joins you in commission
  With the right fortunate soldier, the Marquis of Pescara,
  And the famous Lannoy.
Cardinal.   He that had the honour   5
  Of taking the French king prisoner?
Malateste.   The same.
  Here's a plot drawn for a new fortification
  At Naples.
    [The Cardinal and Malateste stand aside, conversing.]
Ferdinand. This great Count Malateste, I perceive,
  Hath got employment?
Delio.   No employment, my lord;   10
  A marginal note in the muster book that he is
  A voluntary lord.
Ferdinand.   He's no soldier?
Delio. He has worn gunpowder in 's hollow tooth,
  For the toothache.

 III.iii.0.1.] The location is at Rome again, in a room in a palace which is probably an Aragonian family possession. A conference is taking place about military and political operations. The two brothers might be sitting at the head of a large table, the other persons standing around (or possibly sitting at a far end of the table), in attendance but out of earshot unless addressed specifically.

 1–8.] Webster has added to his main source, William Painter's *Palace of Pleasure*; the Cardinal's taking up arms is adapted from Painter's incidental account of Pope Julius II, and the other details garnered from Contarini's *History of Italy*.

 1. *Emperor*] Holy Roman Emperor, Charles V.

 7. *plot*] plan.

 10–12. *No . . . lord*] Delio speaks disparagingly of Malateste as a mere cipher, an afterthought.

 12. *voluntary*] volunteer.

 13–14. *He . . . toothache*] Delio scoffs at Malateste, who, he says, puts the saltpetre in gunpowder to medicinal use only.

Silvio. He comes to the leaguer with a full intent   15
    To eat fresh beef and garlic, means to stay
    Till the scent be gone, and straight return to court.
Delio. He hath read all the late service
    As the City Chronicle relates it,
    And keeps two painters going, only to express   20
    Battles in model.
Ferdinand.   Then he'll fight by the book.
Delio. By the almanac, I think—
    To choose good days, and shun the critical.
    That's his mistress' scarf.
Silvio.   Yes, he protests
    He would do much for that taffeta.   25
Delio. I think he would run away from a battle
    To save it from taking prisoner.
Silvio.   He is horribly afraid
    Gunpowder will spoil the perfume on 't.
Delio. I saw a Dutchman break his pate once
    For calling him pot-gun; he made his head   30
    Have a bore in 't, like a musket.
Silvio. I would he had made a touch-hole to 't.
Delio. He is indeed a guarded sumpter cloth,

---

15. *leaguer*] military camp.
16. *fresh . . . garlic*] food designed to increase martial ardour.
17. *scent*] scent of military excitement, and of garlic.
18. *late service*] recent military operations.
20. *express*] depict.
21. *model*] scale-drawing, ground-plan.
by the book] a common phrase for 'according to rule, in set phrase or manner'; also 'theoretically, rather than practically'.
23. *good*] well-omened.
24. *That's*] Delio points to a scarf that Malateste is wearing.
25. *taffeta*] glossy silk material.
27. *taking*] being taken.
28. *on 't*] of it.
30. *pot-gun*] a child's toy, sometimes called 'pop-gun'; here used, contemptuously, of a braggart, boaster.
he] the Dutchman. (Also in l. 32.)
32. *touch-hole*] i.e. where the charge might be ignited (and so kill off Malateste).
33. Delio.] This speech-prefix is missing in Q, but l. 33 begins a new page, and at the foot of the previous one another compositor did set this prefix as a 'catchword' (used to ensure continuity in making up the book); this means

Only for the remove of the court.

Enter BOSOLA [*and talks with Ferdinand
and the Cardinal in private*].

Pescara. Bosola arrived! What should be the business?   35
    Some falling out amongst the cardinals.
    These factions amongst great men, they are like
    Foxes: when their heads are divided
    They carry fire in their tails, and all the country
    About them goes to wrack for 't.
Silvio.   What's that Bosola?   40
Delio. I knew him in Padua—a fantastical scholar, like such
    who study to know how many knots was in Hercules'
    club, of what colour Achilles' beard was, or whether
    Hector were not troubled with the toothache; he hath
    studied himself half blear-eyed to know the true symme-   45
    try of Caesar's nose by a shoeing-horn: and this he did to
    gain the name of a speculative man.

---

that it was in the second compositor's copy, but was mistakenly missed by
him. The *indeed* in l. 33 suggests that its speaker is agreeing with a previous
speaker.

33–4. *guarded . . . court*] ornamented cloth covering a pack-horse when it
is employed in changing the place of residence of the court.

34.1 S.D.] This entry is at the head of the scene in Q with those for all the
other persons in the scene, following the scribe's regularizing method; however, Bosola is arriving at Rome from Malfi and therefore unlikely to enter
with those who are there already. This edition marks the entry at the latest
possible point, though Bosola might well arrive earlier; he knows that his
news is so important that he must go straight to his master and need not
acknowledge the assembled company. Ferdinand's reaction is a brooding
silence which starts well before it noticed in the dialogue (see ll. 48–9).

37–40.] an allusion to the biblical story of Samson, who tied pairs of foxes
together by their tails and attached firebrands to them; when let loose, they
destroyed the Philistines' harvest (see Judges, 15.4–5).

41–7.] Ambitious young men, like Thomas Overbury (see Introduction to
Revels Student Edition of *W.D.*, pp. 7–8) or Flamineo (see *W.D.*, I.ii.320–
33), came from the universities to seek preferment with 'great men'; a
reputation for being *speculative* (far-seeing, deeply searching, intelligent)
would be a recommendation. Delio's *fantastical* account of Bosola's studies
suggests the envious satire of someone who has not the advantage of a
university education.

41. *Padua*] This 'nursery of Arts' (*Taming of the Shrew*, I.i.2) was one of
the most famous and ancient universities of the time.

Pescara. Mark Prince Ferdinand:
    A very salamander lives in 's eye,
    To mock the eager violence of fire.   50
Silvio. That Cardinal hath made more bad faces with his
    oppression than ever Michael Angelo made good ones; he
    lifts up 's nose, like a foul porpoise before a storm—
Pescara. The Lord Ferdinand laughs.
Delio.   Like a deadly cannon
    That lightens ere it smokes.   55
Pescara. These are your true pangs of death,
    The pangs of life, that struggle with great statesmen—
Delio. In such a deformed silence, witches whisper
    Their charms.
Cardinal. Doth she make religion her riding hood   60
    To keep her from the sun and tempest?
Ferdinand.   That!—
    That damns her. Methinks her fault and beauty,
    Blended together, show like leprosy,
    The whiter the fouler. I make it a question
    Whether her beggarly brats were ever christened.   65
Cardinal. I will instantly solicit the state of Ancona
    To have them banished.
Ferdinand.   You are for Loretto?
    I shall not be at your ceremony; fare you well.—
    Write to the Duke of Malfi, my young nephew

49–50.] Salamanders were supposed to live in *fire*, and fire was emblematic of sexual passion, destruction, or torment.

51. *bad faces*] i.e. those of the Cardinal's victims.

52. *Michael Angelo*] The original plan for Michelangelo's frescos in the Pope's Sistine Chapel required only nine figures to be painted; the final version had three hundred (including those of the damned—hence, perhaps, wordplay here on *bad* and *good*).

53. *lifts . . . storm*] A porpoise was said to play *before a storm*.

lifts up 's nose] a phrase used of either an eager person or a proud and haughty one.

55. *lightens*] i.e. flashes with flame.

58. *deformed*] distorted, ugly.

66. *solicit*] petition, urge.

69–70.] This is the only reference in the play to this son, about whom Webster would have read in his main source, Painter's *Palace of Pleasure*; it seems that elsewhere he overlooked or forgot this circumstance, for the claims of an elder son are ignored when Ferdinand speaks of his hope of

She had by her first husband, and acquaint him   70
With 's mother's honesty.
Bosola.   I will.
Ferdinand.   Antonio!
A slave that only smelled of ink and counters,
And ne'er in 's life looked like a gentleman
But in the audit-time.—Go, go presently,
Draw me out an hundred and fifty of our horse,   75
And meet me at the fort-bridge.   *Exeunt.*

Scene iv

    Enter Two Pilgrims *to the Shrine of Our Lady of Loretto.*

First Pilgrim. I have not seen a goodlier shrine than this,
    Yet I have visited many.
Second Pilgrim. The Cardinal of Aragon
    Is this day to resign his cardinal's hat;
    His sister Duchess likewise is arrived   5
    To pay her vow of pilgrimage. I expect
    A noble ceremony.
First Pilgrim.   No question.—They come.

    Here the ceremony of the Cardinal's *instalment in the habit of*
    a soldier, performed in delivering up his cross, hat, robes, and
    ring at the shrine, and investing him with sword, helmet,
    shield, and spurs. Then ANTONIO, *the* Duchess, *and their*
    Children, *having presented themselves at the shrine, are (by*

'treasure' (IV.ii.284–6), and when Delio enters in the play's last moments
with the eldest son of Antonio and the Duchess (whose survival is Webster's
alteration of Painter's account) to claim the duchy 'In 's mother's right'
(V.v.113).

    71. *honesty*] (1) chastity; (2) fair dealing. Both images are ironic or
sarcastic.

    72. *counters*] disks used in counting; or, possibly, debased, worthless coins.

    74. *presently*] immediately.

    III.iv.0.1.] On the significance of this location, see Introduction. The
following scene is often omitted in performance and may be, in the words of
Q's title-page, one of the 'diverse things printed, that the length of the play
would not bear in the presentment'. It was omitted in Q4 of 1678, which was
published 'as it is now acted at the Duke's Theatre'.

a form of banishment in dumb show expressed towards them
by the Cardinal and the state of Ancona) banished. During all
which ceremony, this ditty is sung, to very solemn music, by
divers Churchmen; *and then exeunt* [*all, except the* Two
Pilgrims].

Arms and honours deck thy story	The author
To thy fame's eternal glory!	disclaims
Adverse fortune ever fly thee;	this ditty 10
No disastrous fate come nigh thee!	to be his.

I alone will sing thy praises,
Whom to honour virtue raises,
And thy study, that divine is,
Bent to martial discipline is.   15
Lay aside all those robes lie by thee;
Crown thy arts with arms, they'll beautify thee.

O worthy of worthiest name, adorned in this manner,
Lead bravely thy forces on under war's warlike banner!
O, mayst thou prove fortunate in all martial courses!   20
Guide thou still, by skill, in arts and forces!
Victory attend thee nigh, whilst Fame sings loud thy pow'rs;

8–23.] The lumbering metre and repetitive and clumsy words provide reasons enough for Webster to add a disclaimer of authorship, as he did when he visited the press during the printing of his play (see Introduction). If the ditty was cobbled together by those responsible for providing music during the various ceremonies of this scene, it is notable that they did nothing to supplement or support the second and third parts of what is, in effect, a dumb show—the vows of the Duchess and her family, and their banishment. The first part of this 'dumb show' will be lengthy in performance (because of the practical details of disrobing and arming) and the second and third sections comparatively short (and in need of subsequent explanation). The 'violence' (l. 36) with which the Cardinal takes the ring from the Duchess's finger must be an action of some considerable size to be seen clearly in this silent mode of drama; the 'noble ceremony' (l. 7) is likely to become suddenly disrupted and awkward at this moment.

12. I . . . praises] I will sing only in your praise.

17. arts] learning.

20. courses] encounters.

21. forces] military, physical strength.

Triumphant conquest crown thy head, and blessings pour down
   show'rs!

First Pilgrim. Here's a strange turn of state! Who would have
      thought
   So great a lady would have matched herself   25
   Unto so mean a person? Yet the Cardinal
   Bears himself much too cruel.
Second Pilgrim.   They are banished.
First Pilgrim. But I would ask what power hath this state
   Of Ancona to determine of a free prince?
Second Pilgrim. They are a free state, sir, and her brother
      showed   30
   How that the Pope, fore-hearing of her looseness,
   Hath seized into th' protection of the church
   The dukedom which she held as dowager.
First Pilgrim. But by what justice?
Second Pilgrim.   Sure, I think by none,
   Only her brother's instigation.   35
First Pilgrim. What was it with such violence he took
   Off from her finger?
Second Pilgrim.   'Twas her wedding ring,
   Which he vowed shortly he would sacrifice
   To his revenge.
First Pilgrim.   Alas, Antonio!
   If that a man be thrust into a well,   40
   No matter who sets hand to 't, his own weight
   Will bring him sooner to th' bottom. Come, let's hence.
   Fortune makes this conclusion general:
   All things do help th' unhappy man to fall.   *Exeunt.*

---

26. *mean*] lowly born.

29. *determine of*] judge, decide concerning.

30.] At this time, Ancona was a semi-independent republic protected by
the papacy.

35. *her brother's*] the Cardinal's.

44.] The line may be rescued from being bathetically obvious if 'help' is
strongly stressed (as the metre suggests it should be).

Scene v

    Enter ANTONIO, Duchess, Children, CARIOLA, Servants.

Duchess. Banished Ancona!
Antonio.   Yes, you see what pow'r
    Lightens in great men's breath.
Duchess.   Is all our train
    Shrunk to this poor remainder?
Antonio.   These poor men,
    Which have got little in your service, vow
    To take your fortune; but your wiser buntings,   5
    Now they are fledged, are gone.
Duchess.   They have done wisely.
    This puts me in mind of death; physicians thus,
    With their hands full of money, use to give o'er
    Their patients.
Antonio.   Right the fashion of the world!
    From decayed fortunes every flatterer shrinks;   10
    Men cease to build where the foundation sinks.
Duchess. I had a very strange dream tonight.
Antonio.   What was 't?
Duchess. Methought I wore my coronet of state,
    And on a sudden all the diamonds
    Were changed to pearls.
Antonio.   My interpretation   15
    Is, you'll weep shortly, for to me the pearls
    Do signify your tears.
Duchess. The birds that live i'th' field
    On the wild benefit of nature live
    Happier than we; for they may choose their mates,   20

    III.v.0.1.] This is the first scene to be located in the open air, outside a palace or shrine; everyone will be tired, dressed for travelling, and no longer in court clothes.

    4–6. *vow . . . gone*] vow to share your fortune, whatever it is; but the wiser birds, now that their feathers are grown, have flown from the nest.

    7–9. *physicians . . . patients*] doctors, once they are paid, abandon their patients.

    9. *Right*] just, exactly.

    19. *benefit*] gift, advantages, rights.

And carol their sweet pleasures to the spring.

Enter BOSOLA [*with a letter*].

Bosola. You are happily o'erta'en.
Duchess.   From my brother?
Bosola. Yes, from the Lord Ferdinand, your brother,
    All love and safety—
Duchess.   Thou dost blanch mischief,
    Wouldst make it white. See, see: like to calm weather   25
    At sea, before a tempest, false hearts speak fair
    To those they intend most mischief.
    (*Reads*) *Send Antonio to me; I want his head in a business.*—
    A politic equivocation!
    He doth not want your counsel, but your head;   30
    That is, he cannot sleep till you be dead.
    And here's another pitfall that's strewed o'er
    With roses; mark it, 'tis a cunning one:
    [*Reads*] *I stand engaged for your husband for several debts at*
    Naples. Let not that trouble him; I had rather have his heart   35
    than his money.
    And I believe so too.
Bosola.   What do you believe?
Duchess. That he so much distrusts my husband's love,
    He will by no means believe his heart is with him
    Until he see it. The devil is not cunning enough   40
    To circumvent us in riddles.
Bosola. Will you reject that noble and free league
    Of amity and love which I present you?
Duchess. Their league is like that of some politic kings,
    Only to make themselves of strength and pow'r   45

---

21. *carol*] sing joyfully.
22. *You . . . o'erta'en*] it is fortunate that I have caught up with you.
24. *blanch*] blanch over, 'whitewash'.
mischief] ill fortune, harm. (Also in l. 27.)
25–6. *calm . . . tempest*] Cf. the proverb, 'After a calm comes a storm'.
29. *politic*] cunning.
31. *he . . . dead*] Cf. the Duchess's last words (IV.ii.235–6).
32. *pitfall*] concealed pit, in which animals or men may be captured.
42. *league*] covenant.
44. *league*] alliance, treaty; also suggesting 'covenant', as in l. 42.

To be our after-ruin: tell them so.

Bosola. [*To Antonio*] And what from you?

Antonio.   Thus tell him: I will not come.

Bosola. And what of this?

Antonio.   My brothers have dispersed
    Bloodhounds abroad, which till I hear are muzzled,
    No truce, though hatched with ne'er such politic skill,   50
    Is safe, that hangs upon our enemies' will.
    I'll not come at them.

Bosola.   This proclaims your breeding.
    Every small thing draws a base mind to fear
    As the adamant draws iron. Fare you well, sir;
    You shall shortly hear from 's.   *Exit.*   55

Duchess. I suspect some ambush.
    Therefore, by all my love, I do conjure you
    To take your eldest son and fly towards Milan.
    Let us not venture all this poor remainder
    In one unlucky bottom.

Antonio.   You counsel safely.   60
    Best of my life, farewell. Since we must part,
    Heaven hath a hand in 't, but no otherwise
    Than as some curious artist takes in sunder
    A clock or watch when it is out of frame,
    To bring 't in better order.   65

Duchess. I know not which is best,
    To see you dead, or part with you.—Farewell, boy;
    Thou art happy that thou hast not understanding
    To know thy misery, for all our wit
    And reading brings us to a truer sense   70

---

46. *after-ruin*] future ruin.

48. *this*] i.e. the letter.

brothers] i.e. brothers-in-law.

52. *come at them*] approach them, come within their reach.

54. *adamant*] loadstone, magnet.

59. *all . . . remainder*] i.e. all we have left; with wordplay on = 'residual interest in a deceased person's estate'.

60. *bottom*] hold, ship; 'venture' (l. 59) was commonly used of a merchant's trading voyage.

63. *curious*] skilful.

68–71.] echoing a Biblical proverb; cf. Ecclesiastes, 1.18: 'For in much wisdom is much grief: and he that increaseth knowledge increaseth sorrow'.

Of sorrow.—In the eternal church, sir,
I do hope we shall not part thus.
Antonio.   O, be of comfort!
Make patience a noble fortitude,
And think not how unkindly we are used:
Man, like to cassia, is proved best, being bruised.   75
Duchess. Must I, like to a slave-born Russian,
Account it praise to suffer tyranny?
And yet, O heaven, thy heavy hand is in 't.
I have seen my little boy oft scourge his top
And compared myself to 't: naught made me e'er   80
Go right but heaven's scourge-stick.
Antonio.   Do not weep:
Heaven fashioned us of nothing, and we strive
To bring ourselves to nothing.—Farewell, Cariola,
And thy sweet armful: if I do never see thee more,
Be a good mother to your little ones,   85
And save them from the tiger. Fare you well.
                                         [*They kiss.*]
Duchess. Let me look upon you once more, for that speech
Came from a dying father.—Your kiss is colder
Than that I have seen an holy anchorite
Give to a dead man's skull.   90
Antonio. My heart is turned to a heavy lump of lead,
With which I sound my danger. Fare you well.
                              Exit[, *with his elder* Son].
Duchess. My laurel is all withered.

---

73. *Make*] regard, consider.

74. *unkindly*] with unnatural cruelty.

75.] proverbial; see *W.D.*, I.i.48–51: 'Perfumes the more they are chafed the more they render / Their pleasing scents, and so affliction / Expresseth virtue, fully whether true, / Or else adulterate'.

78. *heaven*] 'God' may well have been censored from Webster's manuscript here, and again at l. 82 (see Introduction, p. 31).

79. *scourge*] i.e. whip (to make it spin).

90.] A dead man's skull could serve as an aid to meditation when fastening the mind on death.

92. *sound*] (1) measure the depth of (as for a vessel at sea); (2) utter, express.

93.] Although *laurel* was, proverbially, 'ever green', it was supposed to wither on the death of a king.

Cariola. Look, madam, what a troop of armèd men
    Make toward us!

            Enter BOSOLA *with a* Guard, *with vizards.*

Duchess.   O, they are very welcome: 95
    When Fortune's wheel is overcharged with princes,
    The weight makes it move swift. I would have my ruin
    Be sudden.—I am your adventure, am I not?
Bosola. You are: you must see your husband no more—
Duchess. What devil art thou, that counterfeits heaven's
            thunder?   100
Bosola. Is that terrible? I would have you tell me
    Whether is that note worse that frights the silly birds
    Out of the corn, or that which doth allure them
    To the nets? You have hearkened to the last too much.
Duchess. O misery! Like to a rusty o'ercharged cannon,   105
    Shall I never fly in pieces? Come. To what prison?
Bosola. To none.
Duchess.   Whither, then?
Bosola.   To your palace.
Duchess.   I have heard

---

95 S.D. with vizards] Q's entry-direction ('... *Bosola, Souldiers, with Vizards*'), placed at the head of the scene (as all are, throughout the play), is ambiguous: it is not clear whether both Bosola and the soldiers all wear vizards, or only the latter. The Duchess's 'What devil art thou' (l. 100) suggests that she does not recognize Bosola; and 'I'd beat that counterfeit face into thy other' (l. 118) seems to imply she had seen through the facial disguise by this time. However, the direction added by Webster during the printing of the play (see Introduction) reads simply '*Enter Bosola with a Guard*', and no vizards are definitely needed by the dialogue, since 'counterfeit' of l. 118 could refer simply to Bosola's apparent change of sides, already clear from his earlier, undisguised entry.

96. *overcharged*] weighted down. The descent on Fortune's wheel is swifter when princes fall.

98. *your adventure*] i.e. what your business is (cf. l. 60, note); also, perhaps, 'what your (good) luck is'.

102. *note*] sound.

silly] ignorant, lowly (see l. 132, below); or, possibly, Bosola is expressing some pity and so = 'frail, defenceless, innocent'.

104. *You ... much*] i.e. you have succumbed to temptation and so are caught.

105. *o'ercharged*] loaded with more gunpowder than its rusty condition will allow.

That Charon's boat serves to convey all o'er
The dismal lake, but brings none back again.

Bosola. Your brothers mean you safety and pity.

Duchess.   Pity!   110
With such a pity men preserve alive
Pheasants and quails, when they are not fat enough
To be eaten.

Bosola. These are your children?

Duchess.   Yes.

Bosola.   Can they prattle?

Duchess.   No:
But I intend, since they were born accurst,   115
Curses shall be their first language.

Bosola.   Fie, madam,
Forget this base, low fellow.

Duchess.   Were I a man
I'd beat that counterfeit face into thy other.

Bosola. One of no birth—

Duchess.   Say that he was born mean;
Man is most happy when 's own actions   120
Be arguments and examples of his virtue.

Bosola. A barren, beggarly virtue.

Duchess. I prithee, who is greatest, can you tell?
Sad tales befit my woe; I'll tell you one.
A salmon, as she swam unto the sea,   125
Met with a dogfish, who encounters her
With this rough language: 'Why art thou so bold
To mix thyself with our high state of floods,
Being no eminent courtier, but one
That for the calmest and fresh time o'th' year   130

---

108. *Charon*] the ferryman of Hades, who took the souls of the dead over the rivers Styx and Acheron to the infernal regions.

109. *dismal*] The word (from L. *dies mali*, day of evil) retained its original senses of 'fatal, disastrous, terrible'.

118. *counterfeit*] See l. 95 S.D., note, above. The Duchess wishes she could smash Bosola's vizard into his face.

120–1.] Cf. Dedication, ll. 14–15.

121. *arguments*] evidence, proof.

126. *dogfish*] a name given to various small sharks; also applied, opprobiously, to persons.

128. *floods*] water (as opposed to land).

Dost live in shallow rivers, rank'st thyself
With silly smelts and shrimps? And darest thou
Pass by our dog-ship, without reverence?'
'O', quoth the salmon, 'sister, be at peace:
Thank Jupiter we both have passed the net!   135
Our value never can be truly known
Till in the fisher's basket we be shown;
I'th' market then my price may be the higher,
Even when I am nearest to the cook and fire.'
So, to great men, the moral may be stretched: 140
Men oft are valued high when th'are most wretch'd.
But come; whither you please. I am armed 'gainst
   misery,
Bent to all sways of the oppressor's will.
There's no deep valley but near some great hill.   *Exeunt.*

---

132. *smelts*] small fish, sparlings; also used of simpletons.

133. *our dog-ship*] a ludicrous honorific title, on the model of 'my lordship'.

143. *Bent to*] (1) determined to withstand; (2) yielding to. See next note.

144.] The line is ambiguous: it might be an argument for 'safety first' or the passive acceptance of misfortune; but it might, on the contrary, be an encouragement of pride or a counsel for biding one's time, in the knowledge that fortune will turn. Either of the latter meanings would be in keeping with ll. 141 and 143 above; and all, perhaps, with l. 6 of the first scene of the next act.

Act IV

Scene i

Enter FERDINAND *and* BOSOLA.

Ferdinand. How doth our sister Duchess bear herself
    In her imprisonment?
Bosola.   Nobly. I'll describe her:
    She's sad, as one long used to 't, and she seems
    Rather to welcome the end of misery
    Than shun it—a behaviour so noble   5
    As gives a majesty to adversity.
    You may discern the shape of loveliness
    More perfect in her tears than in her smiles;
    She will muse four hours together, and her silence,
    Methinks, expresseth more than if she spake.   10
Ferdinand. Her melancholy seems to be fortified
    With a strange disdain.
Bosola.   'Tis so, and this restraint,
    Like English mastiffs that grow fierce with tying,
    Makes her too passionately apprehend
    Those pleasures she's kept from.
Ferdinand.   Curse upon her!   15
    I will no longer study in the book

IV.1.0.1.] Bosola promised to convey the Duchess to her 'palace'
(III.v.107), and talk of her 'chamber' and 'lodging' (IV.i.26, 128, and IV.ii.3)
could imply that he has done so (cf. 'lodgings', II.iii.3). Thus 'imprisonment'
(l. 2) would mean 'house arrest'. However, Webster makes no dramatic point
of such a return, and '*This* is a prison?' (IV.ii.11) does not sound like a
question about familiar surroundings. The Duchess was perhaps right to
assume that she was to be taken to some unknown prison (see III.v.106). The
location is dark, and it is night-time; lights are burning on stage (see ll. 24–
30, especially l. 24).
   7. *shape*] image, picture.
   14. *apprehend*] imagine.

Of another's heart. Inform her what I told you.   *Exit.*

                Enter Duchess *and* CARIOLA.

Bosola. All comfort to your grace!
Duchess.   I will have none.
    Pray thee, why dost thou wrap thy poisoned pills
    In gold and sugar?   20
Bosola. Your elder brother, the Lord Ferdinand,
    Is come to visit you, and sends you word,
    'Cause once he rashly made a solemn vow
    Never to see you more, he comes i'th' night;
    And prays you, gently, neither torch nor taper   25
    Shine in your chamber. He will kiss your hand
    And reconcile himself; but, for his vow,
    He dares not see you.
Duchess.   At his pleasure;
    Take hence the lights.   [*Bosola removes lights.*]

                [*Enter* FERDINAND.]

                    He's come.
Ferdinand.   Where are you?
Duchess.   Here, sir.
Ferdinand. This darkness suits you well.   30
Duchess. I would ask you pardon.
Ferdinand.   You have it;
    For I account it the honourabl'st revenge,
    Where I may kill, to pardon. Where are your cubs?
Duchess. Whom?
Ferdinand. Call them your children;   35
    For though our national law distinguish bastards

19–20. *wrap . . . sugar*] Cf. *W.D.*, III.ii.190–1: 'I discern poison, / Under
your gilded pills'. When used of ill-tasting but beneficial pills, the idea was
proverbial.
    21. *elder*] In Webster's source, Ferdinand is older than his sister; but in the
play the two are twins (see IV.ii.266–8) and the Cardinal is the younger of the
two brothers.
    31–3. *I . . . pardon*] Proverbially, 'To pardon is divine revenge'; but
Ferdinand's next words show that he does not offer restitution of trust,
understanding, or love. In effect, he threatens her with a lifetime of being
ostracized and left to suffer her loss and shame. See also l. 110, below.

From true legitimate issue, compassionate nature
Makes them all equal.

Duchess.   Do you visit me for this?
You violate a sacrament o'th' church
Shall make you howl in hell for 't.

Ferdinand.   It had been well   40
Could you have lived thus always, for indeed
You were too much i'th' light. But no more;
I come to seal my peace with you. Here's a hand
                    Gives her a dead man's hand.
To which you have vowed much love; the ring upon 't
You gave.

Duchess.   I affectionately kiss it.   45

Ferdinand. Pray do, and bury the print of it in your heart.
I will leave this ring with you for a love token,
And the hand, as sure as the ring; and do not doubt
But you shall have the heart too. When you need a
     friend,
Send it to him that owed it; you shall see   50
Whether he can aid you.

Duchess.   You are very cold.
I fear you are not well after your travel.—
Hah! Lights!—O, horrible!

Ferdinand.   Let her have lights enough.
                                        Exit.

Duchess. What witchcraft doth he practise that he hath left
A dead man's hand here?—   55

> *Here is discovered, behind a traverse,*
> *the artificial figures of* ANTONIO *and his* children,
> *appearing as if they were dead.*

---

39. *sacrament o'th' church*] i.e. marriage.

40. *Shall*] which shall.

42. *too . . . light*] i.e. too exposed, not sufficiently sheltered; but *too much* suggests also a common quibble, as in *Merchant of Venice*, V.i.129–30: 'Let me give light, but let me not be light [i.e., wanton]; / For a light wife doth make a heavy husband'.

50. *owed*] owned.

55.1 S.D. Here . . . traverse] 'Discover' was often used in Renaissance stage directions to indicate the opening of some curtained acting area; 'traverse' was used of curtains or screen across a room, hall, or stage.

Bosola. Look you, here's the piece from which 'twas ta'en.
    He doth present you this sad spectacle
    That, now you know directly they are dead,
    Hereafter you may wisely cease to grieve
    For that which cannot be recoverèd.   60
Duchess. There is not between heaven and earth one wish
    I stay for after this: it wastes me more
    Than were 't my picture, fashioned out of wax,
    Stuck with a magical needle and then buried
    In some foul dunghill; and yon 's an excellent property   65
    For a tyrant, which I would account mercy.
Bosola. What's that?
Duchess. If they would bind me to that lifeless trunk,
    And let me freeze to death.
Bosola.   Come, you must live.
Duchess. That's the greatest torture souls feel in hell—   70
    In hell, that they must live, and cannot die.
    Portia, I'll new-kindle thy coals again,
    And revive the rare and almost dead example
    Of a loving wife.
Bosola.   O, fie! Despair? Remember
    You are a Christian.
Duchess.   The church enjoins fasting: 75
    I'll starve myself to death.
Bosola.   Leave this vain sorrow.
    Things being at the worst begin to mend;

---

58. *directly*] plainly, immediately.

62–5. *it wastes . . . dunghill*] Wax dolls, stuck with needles or pins (representing daggers stuck into the heart), were thus buried in the belief that as the wax is consumed (*wastes*) in the heat of the *dunghill*, so will the person it represents.

65. *property*] tool, device.

66. *which . . . mercy*] i.e. which I would account a release from suffering by being allowed to die.

68–9. *bind . . . death*] This punishment was illustrated in emblem books to symbolize ill-matched marriages.

72. *Portia*] When the hopes of her husband were shattered after the assassination of Caesar, Portia killed herself by putting live coals into her mouth which she then kept shut until she died.

76. *starve . . . death*] Some churchmen argued that this form of suicide was, in some circumstances, permissible.

    The bee, when he hath shot his sting into your hand,
    May then play with your eyelid.
Duchess. Good comfortable fellow,   80
    Persuade a wretch that's broke upon the wheel
    To have all his bones new set; entreat him live
    To be executed again. Who must despatch me?
    I account this world a tedious theatre,
    For I do play a part in 't 'gainst my will.   85
Bosola. Come, be of comfort; I will save your life.
Duchess. Indeed, I have not leisure to tend so small a
    business.
Bosola. Now, by my life, I pity you.
Duchess.   Thou art a fool, then,
    To waste thy pity on a thing so wretched
    As cannot pity itself. I am full of daggers.   90
    Puff! Let me blow these vapours from me.

Enter Servant.

    What are you?
Servant.   One that wishes you long life.
Duchess. I would thou wert hanged for the horrible curse
    Thou hast given me.   [*Exit* Servant.]
                    I shall shortly grow one

---

78. *shot*] discharged. Bees that have lost their sting have done their worst.

80.] The Duchess nowhere recognizes Bosola in this scene (see especially l. 88, below), and Webster probably intended him to be unrecognizable in the guise of a gaoler. Such protection would help him to speak more *comfortable* words than would be possible in continuation of his earlier relationship to the Duchess; it would also explain why the Duchess does not address him by name. In any case, *comfortable* is dramatically ironic, since he is her gaoler and executioner.

81. *wheel*] an instrument of torture used to pull the body apart.

90. *daggers*] i.e. mental afflictions, penetrating pains.

91. *vapours*] Q reads 'vipers', which makes no sense with 'Puff' and 'blow'. If the original manuscript read 'vapors' (a common seventeenth-century spelling), a misreading of its 'secretary' script could easily produce 'vipers'. *Vapours* may be a variation of 'mist', as used by Webster of perplexities at the time of death; see IV.ii.187 and note. He used *vapours* = 'insubstantial things, thoughts' in *A Monumental Column* (1613), a poem with many echoes of *The Duchess.*

94 S.D.] The servant may slip away at any time when least noticeable, or he may make a clumsy retreat in the face of the Duchess's reproof.

Of the miracles of pity.—I'll go pray. No,   95
   I'll go curse.
Bosola.   O, fie!
Duchess.   I could curse the stars—
Bosola.   O, fearful!
Duchess. And those three smiling seasons of the year
   Into a Russian winter, nay, the world
   To its first chaos.
Bosola. Look you, the stars shine still.
Duchess.   O, but you must   100
   Remember, my curse hath a great way to go.—
   Plagues, that make lanes through largest families,
   Consume them!
Bosola.   Fie, lady!
Duchess.   Let them, like tyrants,
   Never be remembered but for the ill they have done;
   Let all the zealous prayers of mortified   105
   Churchmen forget them!
Bosola.   O, uncharitable!
Duchess. Let heaven, a little while, cease crowning martyrs,
   To punish them!
   Go, howl them this, and say I long to bleed:
   It is some mercy, when men kill with speed.   *Exit.*   110

[*Enter* FERDINAND.]

Ferdinand. Excellent, as I would wish; she's plagued in art.
   These presentations are but framed in wax
   By the curious master in that quality,

---

95. *miracles*] marvels, outstanding examples.

97. *those . . . year*] spring, summer, and autumn.

102–3. *Plagues . . . them*] The image of cannon-shot is clearer in Webster's probable source for this (and for other details in this play), George Chapman's *Penitential Psalms* (1612): 'Wars that make lanes through whole posterities'; and in the same writer's *Bussy D'Ambois*: 'a murdering piece, making lanes in armies'.

105. *mortified*] i.e. emaciated by penance and self-discipline; or, perhaps, 'dead to the world'.

112–14. *These . . . Lauriola*] Wax effigies of the dead were placed on their coffins in funeral processions of the great; a collection of them could be viewed in Westminster Abbey.

curious] expert, ingenious, scrupulous.

quality] craft, art.

    Vincentio Lauriola, and she takes them
    For true substantial bodies.   115
Bosola. Why do you do this?
Ferdinand.   To bring her to despair.
Bosola. Faith, end here,
    And go no farther in your cruelty.
    Send her a penitential garment to put on
    Next to her delicate skin, and furnish her   120
    With beads and prayerbooks.
Ferdinand.   Damn her! That body of hers,
    While that my blood ran pure in 't, was more worth
    Than that which thou wouldst comfort, called a soul.
    I will send her masques of common courtesans,
    Have her meat served up by bawds and ruffians,   125
    And, 'cause she'll needs be mad, I am resolved
    To remove forth the common hospital
    All the mad folk, and place them near her lodging;
    There let them practise together, sing, and dance,
    And act their gambols to the full o'th' moon.   130
    If she can sleep the better for it, let her—
    Your work is almost ended.
Bosola. Must I see her again?
Ferdinand.   Yes.
Bosola.   Never.
Ferdinand.   You must.
Bosola. Never in mine own shape;

---

    114. *Vincentio Lauriola*] Webster probably invented this name.

    121–3. *That body . . . soul*] for Webster's contemporaries a starkly (or ob-
sessively) irreligious statement. The church taught that the *body* was only a
temporary house for the *soul* while on earth; sometimes it was called the
soul's prison or other cages of much 'less *worth*' (see IV.ii.123–32).

    127. *forth*] forth from.

    129–30.] These lines continue Ferdinand's reaction to Bosola's evocation
of the Duchess's 'delicate skin' (l. 120). Having damned her for 'that body of
hers', and having thought of sending prostitutes and bawds to entertain and
wait upon her, he now brings in the 'mad folk' with a series of sexually
charged words: *practise together* (cf. *W.D.*, II.i.110), *act, gambols, moon*. He
then imagines his sister in bed at night.

    130. *full o'th' moon*] Madness was said to be influenced by the moon, its
effect being strongest when it was full.

That's forfeited by my intelligence   135
And this last cruel lie. When you send me next,
The business shall be comfort.
Ferdinand.   Very likely!
Thy pity is nothing of kin to thee. Antonio
Lurks about Milan; thou shalt shortly thither
To feed a fire as great as my revenge,   140
Which ne'er will slack till it have spent his fuel.
Intemperate agues make physicians cruel.   *Exeunt.*

Scene ii

Enter Duchess *and* CARIOLA.

Duchess. What hideous noise was that?
Cariola.   'Tis the wild consort
Of madmen, lady, which your tyrant brother
Hath placed about your lodging. This tyranny,
I think, was never practised till this hour.
Duchess. Indeed, I thank him: nothing but noise and folly   5
Can keep me in my right wits, whereas reason
And silence make me stark mad. Sit down;
Discourse to me some dismal tragedy.
Cariola. O, 'twill increase your melancholy.
Duchess.   Thou art deceived;
To hear of greater grief would lessen mine.—   10
This is a prison?
Cariola.   Yes, but you shall live

135.] i.e. 'She will not listen to me because she knows I have spied against her and acted on your behalf'. However, Bosola may be protecting himself from being too intimate with the Duchess because she is already arousing his genuine pity; see 'cruel' in the next line, which seems to derive from his own feelings, rather than paid loyalty to Ferdinand.

141. *his*] its.

142. agues] fevers. (The saying is proverbial.)

IV.ii.0.1 S.D.] The location is unchanged from that of the previous scene.

1. *consort*] company; with an ironical quibble on *consort* = 'group of musicians', 'harmonious music', and on 'noise' of the same line = 'music', 'band of musicians'.

To shake this durance off.

Duchess.   Thou art a fool.
    The robin redbreast and the nightingale
    Never live long in cages.

Cariola.   Pray, dry your eyes.
    What think you of, madam?

Duchess.   Of nothing;   15
    When I muse thus, I sleep.

Cariola. Like a madman, with your eyes open?

Duchess. Dost thou think we shall know one another
    In th'other world?

Cariola.   Yes, out of question.

Duchess. O, that it were possible we might   20
    But hold some two days' conference with the dead!
    From them I should learn somewhat, I am sure,
    I never shall know here. I'll tell thee a miracle:
    I am not mad yet, to my cause of sorrow.
    Th' heaven o'er my head seems made of molten brass,   25
    The earth of flaming sulphur, yet I am not mad.
    I am acquainted with sad misery,
    As the tanned galley slave is with his oar;
    Necessity makes me suffer constantly,
    And custom makes it easy.—Who do I look like now?   30

Cariola. Like to your picture in the gallery,
    A deal of life in show, but none in practice;
    Or rather like some reverend monument
    Whose ruins are even pitied.

Duchess.   Very proper;

---

12. *durance*] (1) imprisonment; (2) duration; (3) endurance.

25-6. *Th' heaven . . . sulphur*] an echo of a biblical curse in the Old Testament, pronounced upon those who 'will not hearken unto the voice of the Lord thy god': 'the heaven that is over thy head shall be brass, and the earth that is under thee shall be iron'. *Sulphur*, which here takes the place of 'iron', is associated with hell (cf., for example, *Lear*, IV.vi.128–30: 'There's hell, there's darkness, there is the sulphurous pit, burning, scalding, stench, consumption').

28. *tanned*] darkened and hardened by exposure to the sun.

32. *A deal . . . show*] rather lifelike in appearance.

33. *monument*] statue, effigy.

34. *pitied*] with wordplay on 'pitted' = disfigured with scars, worn away.
proper] appropriate; and also, ironically, 'excellent'.

And Fortune seems only to have her eyesight   35
To behold my tragedy.—How now!
What noise is that?

Enter Servant.

Servant.   I am come to tell you
Your brother hath intended you some sport.
A great physician, when the Pope was sick
Of a deep melancholy, presented him   40
With several sorts of madmen, which wild object,
Being full of change and sport, forced him to laugh,
And so th' imposthume broke: the self-same cure
The Duke intends on you.
Duchess.   Let them come in.
Servant. There's a mad lawyer, and a secular priest;   45
A doctor that hath forfeited his wits
By jealousy; an astrologian
That in his works said such a day o'th' month
Should be the day of doom, and, failing of 't,
Ran mad; an English tailor, crazed i'th' brain   50
With the study of new fashion; a gentleman usher
Quite beside himself with care to keep in mind
The number of his lady's salutations,
Or 'How do you', she employed him in each morning;
A farmer, too, an excellent knave in grain,   55
Mad 'cause he was hindered transportation.
And let one broker that's mad loose to these,
You'd think the devil were among them.

35–6. *Fortune . . . tragedy*] i.e. The 'blind' (I.i.494–5) goddess Fortune is
forced to regard my misfortune as outreaching all others.

42. *change and sport*] variety and amusement.

43. *imposthume*] abscess.

45. *secular*] i.e. living 'in the world', not in monastic seclusion.

49. *day of doom*] day of final judgement of the world before God.

55. *knave in grain*] a common phrase for a thorough rogue (*in grain* =
'dyed fast'); with a quibble on the grain trade.

56. *hindered transportation*] probably an allusion to regulations allowing the
export of grain only when its price fell below a certain level. On 18 January
1613, a proclamation forbade the export (*transportation*) because of a peculiar
shortage.

57. *broker*] used of a variety of trades, as pedlar, dealer, pawnbroker,
agent, procurer.

Duchess. Sit, Cariola.—Let them loose when you please,
For I am chained to endure all your tyranny.   60

Enter Madmen.

Here, by a Madman, *this song is sung, to a dismal kind of music.*

> *O, let us howl some heavy note,*
>   *Some deadly doggèd howl,*
> *Sounding as from the threat'ning throat*
>   *Of beasts and fatal fowl!*
> *As ravens, screech-owls, bulls, and bears,*   65
>   *We'll bill and bawl our parts,*
> *Till irksome noise have cloyed your ears*
>   *And corrosived your hearts.*
> *At last whenas our choir wants breath,*
>   *Our bodies being blest,*   70
> *We'll sing like swans, to welcome death,*
>   *And die in love and rest.*

First Madman. Doomsday not come yet? I'll draw it nearer by

---

60. *chained*] as opposed to 'loose' in the previous line. Madmen were frequently controlled by being bound and only the most violent were *chained*.

60.2 S.D.] On the masque-like elements of this scene, see Introduction, p. 13. The music for the song has survived in three manuscripts, one of which ascribes it to Robert Johnson (*c.* 1582–1633). Stylistically an example of the declamatory songs composed in England at this time, it is marked as a 'mad song' by sinister inflections on 'howl' and a wayward harmonic twist at the 'threat'ning throat / Of beasts . . .' followed by wide leaps for 'ravens, screech-owls . . . bawl'. An edited transcript of the earliest manuscript can be found in Appendix II of the Revels Plays edition of the play.

66. bill] utter through bill or beak (on the analogy of 'mouth' = 'to declaim'). Q2 and two of the music manuscripts read 'bell'; but, like 'bawl', this is appropriate to animals, and so would lose the opposition between birds and beasts which is a repeated feature of the song.

67. irksome] physically painful.

68. corrosived] corroded, fretted, vexed.

71.] Swans were said to exchange their harsh cries for a sweet song as they were about to die.

73. First Madman] His first speech characterizes him as the Astrologer, but at l. 93 he sounds like the Lawyer, and at l. 100 he might be any of the eight. The second Madman is not as clearly characterized; the third is the Priest for his first three or four speeches; and the fourth is consistently the Doctor. Probably Webster numbered the speeches 1 to 4 to show where each begins and ends and left both characterized and uncharacterized to be allocated among the Madmen according to the actors available at each performance.

a perspective, or make a glass that shall set all the
world on fire upon an instant. I cannot sleep; my pillow   75
is stuffed with a litter of porcupines.

Second Madman. Hell is a mere glass-house, where the devils
are continually blowing up women's souls on hollow
irons, and the fire never goes out.

Third Madman. I will lie with every woman in my parish the   80
tenth night: I will tithe them over, like haycocks.

Fourth Madman. Shall my pothecary outgo me, because I am
a cuckold? I have found out his roguery: he makes alum
of his wife's urine, and sells it to Puritans that have sore
throats with overstraining.   85

First Madman. I have skill in heraldry.

Second Madman. Hast?

First Madman. You do give for your crest a woodcock's head
with the brains picked out on 't; you are a very ancient
gentleman.   90

Third Madman. Greek is turned Turk; we are only to be saved
by the Helvetian translation.

---

74. *perspective*] optical instrument, here a magnifying glass or telescope.

glass] a burning-glass, a lens used to make fire by concentrating the sun's
beams on a very small area (i.e. *not* 'all the world').

77–9. *glass-house . . . out*] There was a glass-making furnace near the
Blackfriars. Blown glass held something like the same fascination for Webster
as that which Hieronymus Bosch shows in his paintings; at II.ii.6–12, its
shape is likened to a woman's pregnant belly and, in *W.D.*, I.ii.136–9, a
glass-factory is associated with lust. Here the Second Madman probably
envisioned a soul as a naked body, as in pictorial representations of hell.

81. *tithe*] decimate; suggesting also the paying of *tithes*, or tenths, to the
church.

haycocks] conical haystacks.

82. *pothecary*] apothecary, druggist.

84–5. *Puritans . . . overstraining*] i.e. Puritans who have sung too many
psalms too fervently.

88–90.] For the granting of arms, see III.ii.301, note. To *give* is to display
heraldically; *ancient* implies either that the Second Madman has no need to
invent a coat of arms, or that he has been the fool represented in his crest for
a very long time. A *woodcock* is a bird easily caught in snares and nets, hence
a fool or dupe.

91–2.] The Genevan (Helvetian) Bible of 1560 had a strong Puritan bias in
its translation and notes. To the Calvinist Third Madman, any other translation (such as the Authorized Version of 1611 or the Douay version of 1609–
10) turns the Greek New Testament into heathen Turk.

only . . . saved] The title-page of the Geneva New Testament had Exodus,

First Madman. Come on, sir, I will lay the law to you.
Second Madman. O, rather lay a corrosive; the law will eat to
    the bone.   95
Third Madman. He that drinks but to satisfy nature is
    damned.
Fourth Madman. If I had my glass here, I would show a sight
    should make all the women here call me mad doctor.
First Madman. What's he, a rope-maker?   100
                [*Points at Third Madman.*]
Second Madman. No, no, no, a snuffling knave that, while
    he shows the tombs, will have his hand in a wench's
    placket.
Third Madman. Woe to the caroche that brought home my
    wife from the masque at three o'clock in the morning! It   105
    had a large featherbed in it.
Fourth Madman. I have pared the devil's nails forty times,
    roasted them in raven's eggs, and cured agues with them.
Third Madman. Get me three hundred milch-bats to make
    possets, to procure sleep.   110
Fourth Madman. All the college may throw their caps at

14.13 as a motto: 'Fear ye not, stand still, and behold the salvation of the
Lord, which he will show to you this day.'

93. *lay*] expound.

94. *corrosive*] corrosive, or caustic, medicine; often used, figuratively, for
either 'grief, annoyance' or 'sharp remedy'.

96–7.] i.e. only drunks are blessed.

98. *glass*] a perspective glass, as at l. 74.

100. *rope-maker*] a trade closely allied to the hangman's.

103. *placket*] petticoat, or opening in a skirt.

104. *caroche*] a stately kind of coach.

106. *featherbed*] This mad fantasy touches on the fact that coaches were
sometimes luxuriously equipped.

107. *pared . . . nails*] a proverbial saying, similar to 'clipping his wings'.

108. *agues*] fevers.

109. *milch-bats*] The mad Doctor supposes that bats will, as nocturnal
creatures, yield milk suitable for narcotics.

110. *possets*] drinks of hot milk curdled with ale or wine, and with added
sugar, spices, etc.

111. *college*] community of clergmen or learned men.

111–12. *throw . . . me*] pursue, do their utmost against me.

me; I have made a soap-boiler costive—it was my
masterpiece.

Here the dance, consisting of eight Madmen, *with music
answerable thereunto; after which* BOSOLA, *like an old man,
enters [and the* Madmen *leave].*

Duchess. Is he mad too?
Servant.   Pray, question him. I'll leave you.
                                             [*Exit.*]
Bosola. I am come to make thy tomb.
Duchess.   Hah, my tomb!   115
      Thou speak'st as if I lay upon my death-bed,
      Gasping for breath: dost thou perceive me sick?
Bosola. Yes, and the more dangerously, since thy sickness is
      insensible.
Duchess. Thou art not mad, sure—dost know me?   120
Bosola. Yes.
Duchess. Who am I?
Bosola. Thou art a box of worm-seed; at best, but a salvatory
      of green mummy. What's this flesh? A little crudded
      milk, fantastical puff-paste. Our bodies are weaker than   125
      those paper prisons boys use to keep flies in; more con-
      temptible, since ours is to preserve earthworms. Didst
      thou ever see a lark in a cage? Such is the soul in the
      body; this world is like her little turf of grass, and the

---

112. *made . . . costive*] A soap-maker (*soap-boiler*) was seldom constipated
or *costive*, because soap was an ingredient in suppositories designed to loosen
the bowels.

119. *insensible*] imperceptible.

123. *worm-seed*] The dried flower-heads of this plant were used as a
medicine against intestinal worms. There is a quibble on *seed* = 'origin,
germ'.

   salvatory] box for holding ointment.

124. *green mummy*] A medicine was prepared from mummies; *green* is
presumably a quibble to suggest a 'living' corpse, or flesh that is not 'ripe'
enough to be mummy.

   crudded] curdled.

125. *fantastical puff-paste*] a fragile and eccentric confection, like an airy
pastry.

127. *preserve*] keep alive.

129. *turf of grass*] placed in the cage to supply a small sample of the lark's
natural habitat.

heaven o'er our heads, like her looking-glass, only gives   130
us a miserable knowledge of the small compass of our
prison.

Duchess. Am not I thy Duchess?

Bosola. Thou art some great woman, sure, for riot begins to
sit on thy forehead, clad in grey hairs, twenty years sooner   135
than on a merry milkmaid's. Thou sleepest worse than if
a mouse should be forced to take up her lodging in a cat's
ear; a little infant that breeds its teeth, should it lie with
thee, would cry out as if thou wert the more unquiet
bedfellow.   140

Duchess. I am Duchess of Malfi still.

Bosola. That makes thy sleeps so broken.
   Glories, like glow-worms, afar off shine bright,
   But, looked to near, have neither heat nor light.

Duchess. Thou art very plain.   145

Bosola. My trade is to flatter the dead, not the living; I am a
tomb-maker.

Duchess. And thou comest to make my tomb?

Bosola. Yes.

Duchess. Let me be a little merry. Of what stuff wilt thou   150
make it?

Bosola. Nay, resolve me first, of what fashion?

Duchess. Why, do we grow fantastical in our death-bed? Do
we affect fashion in the grave?

Bosola. Most ambitiously. Princes' images on their tombs do   155
not lie, as they were wont, seeming to pray up to heaven,
but with their hands under their cheeks, as if they died of
the toothache; they are not carved with their eyes fixed
upon the stars, but as their minds were wholly bent

---

134. *riot*] the disorder (of age).
136. *merry milkmaid's*] proverbially fair, innocent, and carefree.
138. *breeds its teeth*] has new teeth coming in.
143–4.] repeated from *W.D.*, V.i.41–2.
looked to] looked at.
152. *resolve*] satisfy, explain to.
154. *affect*] crave, like to use.
155–61.] This fashion in tomb-making, found in England by the 1560s,
may have reflected Etruscan style in which the effigies lay at table rather than
praying.

upon the world, the selfsame way they seem to turn their   160
    faces.
Duchess. Let me know fully therefore the effect
    Of this thy dismal preparation,
    This talk fit for a charnel.
Bosola.   Now I shall.

       Enter Executioners[, *with*] *a coffin, cords, and a bell.*

Here is a present from your princely brothers,   165
    And may it arrive welcome, for it brings
    Last benefit, last sorrow.
Duchess.   Let me see it.—
    I have so much obedience in my blood,
    I wish it in their veins, to do them good.
Bosola. This is your last presence chamber.   170
Cariola. O my sweet lady!
Duchess.   Peace, it affrights not me.
Bosola. I am the common bellman
    That usually is sent to condemned persons
    The night before they suffer.
Duchess.   Even now thou said'st
    Thou wast a tomb-maker.
Bosola.   'Twas to bring you   175

---

162. *effect*] purpose.

164.1 S.D. cords] representing, as symbols in a masque, both a wedding ring (cf. l. 248, below) and a 'love knot'. (Cf. *W.D.*, V.iii.175–6, as Bracciano is strangled: 'This is a true-love knot / Sent from the Duke of Florence'.)

167. *benefit*] bestowal of rights, benefaction.

170. *This . . . presence chamber*] an allusion to the location and basic action of the beginning of I.i and II.i; in performance, the grouping of figures on stage may provide a visual echo of the earlier scenes.

172. *common bellman*] In 1605, Robert Dowe or Dove, a Merchant Tailor, founded a charity at the church of St Sepulchre near Newgate prison, to provide a *bellman* to make a speech outside the dungeon of condemned prisoners the night before their execution, and another the next morning as the cart conveying them to Tyburn was stayed outside the church. (The dramatist lived within earshot, almost within sight, of this public spectacle.) The benefactor's purpose was to 'put them in mind of their mortality' and so 'awake their sleepy senses from security, to save their souls from perishing'. The words of both speeches were prescribed and a refrain, to a tolling handbell, was to accompany them: 'Our Lord take mercy upon you all'.

By degrees to mortification. Listen:

> *Hark, now everything is still!*
> *The screech-owl and the whistler shrill*
> *Call upon our dame aloud,*
> *And bid her quickly don her shroud.*   180
> *Much you had of land and rent;*
> *Your length in clay's now competent.*
> *A long war disturbed your mind;*
> *Here your perfect peace is signed.*
> *Of what is 't fools make such vain keeping?*   185
> *Sin their conception, their birth weeping;*
> *Their life a general mist of error,*
> *Their death a hideous storm of terror.*
> *Strew your hair with powders sweet,*
> *Don clean linen, bathe your feet,*   190
> *And (the foul fiend more to check)*
> *A crucifix let bless your neck.*

---

176. *mortification*] (1) a mortifying of the flesh by the practice of austerity; (2) the state of torpor and insensibility immediately preceding death.

Listen] Twelve 'solemn tolls by double strokes' preceded the speech of Mr Dove's bellman (see l. 172, note, above). Bosola probably sounds his bell here, and possibly during the dirge, as each new sentence begins or at the end of lines.

178.] The dirge is antithetical to an epithalamium, which customarily bade such creatures be silent on the wedding night.

whistler] applied to various species, as the widgeon, ring-ouzel, and lapwing; to hear the bird's shrill cry was a foreboding of death.

179. our dame] night.

181. rent] income, revenues.

182. competent] appropriate, sufficient.

184.] i.e. here you are released of your sins by God's covenant and taken into his eternal rest.

185. keeping] defending, attempting to keep.

187. mist] often used by Webster for 'uncertainty' or 'confusion of mind', especially at the time of death: cf. V.v.94, and also *W.D.*, V.vi.259–60, as Flamineo is about to die: 'We confound / Knowledge with knowledge. O, I am in a mist.'

189.] In requiring the Duchess to prepare herself to be laid out for burial, the dirge again echoes an epithalamium; by custom, a bride would *strew* her flowing hair with powder.

192.] i.e. wear a crucifix on a neck-chain to ward off evil.

> *'Tis now full tide 'tween night and day;*
> *End your groan, and come away.*

Cariola. Hence, villains, tyrants, murderers! Alas!   195
    What will you do with my lady?—Call for help.
Duchess. To whom? To our next neighbours? They are mad
    folks.
Bosola. [*To Executioners*] Remove that noise.
Duchess.   Farewell, Cariola.
    In my last will I have not much to give;
    A many hungry guests have fed upon me;   200
    Thine will be a poor reversion.
Cariola. [*To Executioners*]   I will die with her.
Duchess. I pray thee, look thou giv'st my little boy
    Some syrup for his cold, and let the girl
    Say her prayers, ere she sleep.
                [Executioners *force* CARIOLA *off.*]
                    Now what you please—
    What death?
Bosola.   Strangling: here are your executioners.   205
Duchess. I forgive them:
    The apoplexy, catarrh, or cough o'th' lungs
    Would do as much as they do.
Bosola. Doth not death fright you?
Duchess.   Who would be afraid on 't?—
    Knowing to meet such excellent company   210
    In th' other world.
Bosola. Yet, methinks,
    The manner of your death should much afflict you,
    This cord should terrify you?
Duchess.   Not a whit.
    What would it pleasure me to have my throat cut   215
    With diamonds? Or to be smothered
    With cassia? Or to be shot to death with pearls?
    I know death hath ten thousand several doors

193–4.] Here the traditional conclusion of an epithalamium is echoed: as the bride is ushered in to the ardent bridegroom, so the Duchess is summoned to a violent death.

201. *reversion*] right of future possession.

207. *catarrh*] cerebral haemorrhage or apoplexy.

For men to take their exits; and 'tis found
They go on such strange geometrical hinges,   220
You may open them both ways.—Any way, for heaven
    sake,
So I were out of your whispering. Tell my brothers
That I perceive death, now I am well awake,
Best gift is they can give, or I can take.
I would fain put off my last woman's fault: 225
I'd not be tedious to you.
Executioners.   We are ready.
Duchess. Dispose my breath how please you, but my body
    Bestow upon my women, will you?
Executioners.   Yes.
Duchess. Pull, and pull strongly, for your able strength
    Must pull down heaven upon me.—   230
    Yet stay: heaven-gates are not so highly arched
    As princes' palaces; they that enter there
    Must go upon their knees.—[*Kneels.*] Come, violent
        death,
    Serve for mandragora to make me sleep!—
    Go tell my brothers, when I am laid out,   235
    They then may feed in quiet.   *They strangle her.*
Bosola. Where's the waiting-woman?

220–1. *go . . . ways*] i.e. either the door of death yields to your push,
opening away from you, or you pull it open towards yourself, by an act of
your own will.

225–6.] *I . . . you*] The Duchess mocks her murderers by referring to
common proverbial slurs, to the effect that a woman's tongue is 'always in
motion' and is 'the last thing about her that dies'.

234. *mandragora*] mandrake. This is the only occasion when Webster uses
this form or alludes to the plant's narcotic properties. Possibly he was
influenced, as other writers have been, by *Othello*, III.iii.330.

235–6.] At the moment of death, Vittoria expressed her heightened consciousness in wordplay (*W.D.*, V.vi.223–4, 232, and 240–1), and so may the
Duchess: *laid out* = (1) prepared for burial and (in view of the series of
allusions to bridal masques and preparation) for a wedding-night; (2) spent,
expended (usually of money); in view of *feed*, there may be a further pun on
'*lay*ing a table'.

236. *feed in quiet*] alluding to the proverbs: 'A little with quiet is the
only diet' and 'Better enjoy a little with quietness than possess much with
trouble'.

Fetch her. Some other strangle the children.

[Executioners *fetch* CARIOLA,
and one goes to strangle the children.]

Look you, there sleeps your mistress.
Cariola.   O, you are damned
Perpetually for this! My turn is next,   240
Is 't not so ordered?
Bosola.   Yes, and I am glad
You are so well prepared for 't.
Cariola.   You are deceived sir,
I am not prepared for 't. I will not die;
I will first come to my answer, and know
How I have offended.
Bosola. [*To Executioners*] Come, dispatch her.—   245
You kept her counsel, now you shall keep ours.
Cariola. I will not die, I must not, I am contracted
To a young gentleman.
Executioner.   Here's your wedding ring.
Cariola. Let me but speak with the Duke: I'll discover
Treason to his person.
Bosola.   Delays!—Throttle her.   250
Executioner. She bites, and scratches!
Cariola.   If you kill me now
I am damned; I have not been at confession
This two years.
Bosola.   When?
Cariola.   I am quick with child.
Bosola.   Why then,
Your credit's saved. [*The Executioners strangle Cariola.*]
Bear her into th' next room;

238.1 S.D.] The children are probably strangled offstage: cf. 'this' of
l. 255, below, and Q's S.D. two lines later.
244. *come . . . answer*] make a legal defence.
253. *When?*] When are my orders to be obeyed?
quick] pregnant.
254. *Your credit's saved*] i.e. your death will spare you the shame of bearing
an illegitimate child. (Said mockingly.)

Let this lie still.

[*Exeunt* Executioners *with the body of* CARIOLA.]

Enter FERDINAND.

Ferdinand.   Is she dead?
Bosola.   She is what   255
    You'd have her. But here begin your pity—
              Shows the Children strangled.
    Alas, how have these offended?
Ferdinand.   The death
    Of young wolves is never to be pitied.
Bosola. Fix your eye here.
Ferdinand.   Constantly.
Bosola.   Do you not weep?
    Other sins only speak; murder shrieks out;   260
    The element of water moistens the earth,
    But blood flies upwards and bedews the heavens.
Ferdinand. Cover her face; mine eyes dazzle; she died young.
Bosola. I think not so; her infelicity
    Seemed to have years too many.   265
Ferdinand. She and I were twins;
    And, should I die this instant, I had lived
    Her time to a minute.
Bosola.   It seems she was born first:
    You have bloodily approved the ancient truth
    That kindred commonly do worse agree   270
    Than remote strangers.
Ferdinand.   Let me see her face again.—

257–8. *The death . . . pitied*] rewording the proverb: 'The death of a young wolf does never come too soon'; and, perhaps, 'The death of wolves is the safety of the sheep'.

260–2.] While proverbial in form and effect, the allusion is to several sayings, rather than a particular one. Perhaps the biblical story of Cain and Abel is also alluded to; see Genesis, 4.10: 'The voice of thy brother's blood crieth unto me from the ground'.

263. *she died young*] There may be an allusion to the proverb, 'The good die young': if so, Ferdinand's reaction to her death would, from its very first moments, include a response to her 'innocence' (l. 277). Another form of the proverb, 'Those that God loves do not live long', suggests, rather, an acceptance of Fate; however this idea is not reflected elsewhere in this scene.

264–5.] i.e. No, she lived a very long time as measured in unhappiness.
269. *approved*] confirmed.

Why didst not thou pity her? What an excellent
Honest man mightst thou have been
If thou hadst borne her to some sanctuary!
Or, bold in a good cause, opposed thyself   275
With thy advancèd sword above thy head
Between her innocence and my revenge!
I bade thee, when I was distracted of my wits,
Go kill my dearest friend, and thou hast done 't.
For let me but examine well the cause: 280
What was the meanness of her match to me?
Only, I must confess, I had a hope,
Had she continued widow, to have gained
An infinite mass of treasure by her death;
And that was the main cause.—Her marriage!—   285
That drew a stream of gall quite through my heart.
For thee (as we observe in tragedies
That a good actor many times is cursed
For playing a villain's part), I hate thee for 't,
And, for my sake, say thou hast done much ill well.   290

Bosola. Let me quicken your memory, for I perceive
You are falling into ingratitude: I challenge
The reward due to my service.

Ferdinand.   I'll tell thee
What I'll give thee—

Bosola.   Do.

Ferdinand.   I'll give thee a pardon
For this murder.

Bosola.   Hah?

Ferdinand.   Yes; and 'tis   295

---

274. *sanctuary*] church where the Duchess would have been protected from arrest.

276. *advancèd*] held aloft.

280–6.] A break in sense (and the actor's delivery) seems inevitable before and after *Her marriage!* in l. 285; the only alternative is emendation. The hope of an *infinite* treasure is probably a spurious explanation: either a conscious trick to deceive Bosola, or an instinctive attempt to displace the tender feeling exposed by *dearest friend* (l. 279) or the still deeper feelings of guilt. However, the *infinite treasure* might allude, in Ferdinand's mind alone, to the possession of his sister's body—in the only way that he could possess it. A further abrupt change follows as Ferdinand veers again, to attack the only person on whom he can vent his feelings.

291. *quicken*] refresh or, with wordplay, 'give life to'.

The largest bounty I can study to do thee.
By what authority didst thou execute
This bloody sentence?
Bosola.   By yours—
Ferdinand.   Mine? Was I her judge?
Did any ceremonial form of law
Doom her to not-being? Did a complete jury   300
Deliver her conviction up i'th' court?
Where shalt thou find this judgement registered
Unless in hell? See, like a bloody fool,
Th' hast forfeited thy life, and thou shalt die for 't.
Bosola. The office of justice is perverted quite   305
When one thief hangs another.—Who shall dare
To reveal this?
Ferdinand.   O, I'll tell thee:
The wolf shall find her grave, and scrape it up,
Not to devour the corpse, but to discover
The horrid murder.
Bosola.   You, not I, shall quake for 't.   310
Ferdinand. Leave me.
Bosola.   I will first receive my pension.
Ferdinand. You are a villain.
Bosola.   When your ingratitude
Is judge, I am so.
Ferdinand.   O horror!
That not the fear of him which binds the devils
Can prescribe man obedience!   315
Never look upon me more.
Bosola.   Why, fare thee well.
Your brother and yourself are worthy men:
You have a pair of hearts are hollow graves,
Rotten, and rotting others; and your vengeance,
Like two chained bullets, still goest arm in arm.   320
You may be brothers, for treason, like the plague,
Doth take much in a blood. I stand like one

308–10. *The wolf . . . murder*] Wolves were said to uncover the buried bodies of those who had been murdered, and to leave them exposed; cf. *W.D.*, V.iv.104–5.

314.] i.e. that not even fear of God.

320. *chained bullets*] cannon-balls (or half-balls) linked together by a chain; these were used chiefly in naval warfare for destroying masts, rigging, etc.

322. *take . . . blood*] catch a strong hold on a family.

    That long hath ta'en a sweet and golden dream:
    I am angry with myself, now that I wake.
Ferdinand. Get thee into some unknown part o'th' world,   325
    That I may never see thee.
Bosola.   Let me know
    Wherefore I should be thus neglected. Sir,
    I served your tyranny, and rather strove
    To satisfy yourself than all the world;
    And, though I loathed the evil, yet I loved   330
    You that did counsel it, and rather sought
    To appear a true servant than an honest man.
Ferdinand. I'll go hunt the badger by owl-light;
    'Tis a deed of darkness.   *Exit.*
Bosola. He's much distracted. Off, my painted honour!   335
    While with vain hopes our faculties we tire,
    We seem to sweat in ice and freeze in fire.
    What would I do, were this to do again?
    I would not change my peace of conscience
    For all the wealth of Europe.—She stirs; here's life!   340
    Return, fair soul, from darkness, and lead mine
    Out of this sensible hell.—She's warm, she breathes!—
    Upon thy pale lips I will melt my heart
    To store them with fresh colour.—Who's there?
    Some cordial drink!—Alas! I dare not call.   345
    So pity would destroy pity.—Her eye opes,
    And heaven in it seems to ope, that late was shut,
    To take me up to mercy.
Duchess. Antonio!
Bosola.   Yes, madam, he is living—

---

323. *ta'en*] experienced.

333–4.] A *badger* 'is hardly taken, but by devises and gins [traps]' (Topsell, *Four-footed Beasts*, 1607).

owl-light] a fairly common phrase for twilight or evening.

335. *painted*] false, specious; cf. III.ii.282.

336–7.] i.e. in our vain attempts at getting ahead, we prove our own worst enemies and defeat all our efforts.

339.] i.e. if I could recover my peace of conscience by undoing what I have just done, I would not exchange it.

342. *sensible*] palpable.

344. *Who's there?*] Bosola calls out for assistance.

345. *cordial*] heart-restoring.

346. *pity . . . pity*] i.e. calling for help would bring back Ferdinand.

The dead bodies you saw were but feigned statues: 350
He's reconciled to your brothers; the Pope hath wrought
The atonement.
Duchess.   Mercy!   *She dies.*
Bosola. O, she's gone again! There the cords of life broke.
O sacred innocence, that sweetly sleeps
On turtles' feathers, whilst a guilty conscience   355
Is a black register wherein is writ
All our good deeds and bad, a perspective
That shows us hell! That we cannot be suffered
To do good when we have a mind to it!
This is manly sorrow;   360
These tears, I am very certain, never grew
In my mother's milk. My estate is sunk
Below the degree of fear: where were
These penitent fountains while she was living?
O, they were frozen up! Here is a sight   365
As direful to my soul as is the sword
Unto a wretch hath slain his father. Come,
I'll bear thee hence,
And execute thy last will—that's deliver
Thy body to the reverent dispose   370
Of some good women: that the cruel tyrant
Shall not deny me. Then I'll post to Milan,
Where somewhat I will speedily enact
Worth my dejection.
                    Exit[, with the body of the Duchess].

---

352. *atonement*] reconciliation.

353. *cords of life*] sinews or nerves; those of the heart were often spoken of as if they were tangible (e.g. 'Heart-strings').

355. *turtles'*] turtledoves'.

356. *register*] record, account book.

357. *perspective*] optical glass; or, perhaps, 'aspect'. Cf. ll. 74 and 98, above.

358. *suffered*] allowed.

362-3. *My . . . fear*] i.e. I am past fear.

estate] (1) condition (moral, bodily, or mental); (2) fortune, status.

370. *dispose*] disposal.

371-2. *that . . . me*] 'The cruel tyrant shall not deny me that.'

372. *post*] hurry.

374. *dejection*] overthrow, humiliation; dejected spirits.

Act V

Scene i

Enter ANTONIO *and* DELIO.

Antonio. What think you of my hope of reconcilement
    To the Aragonian brethren?
Delio.   I misdoubt it,
    For, though they have sent their letters of safe conduct
    For your repair to Milan, they appear
    But nets to entrap you. The Marquis of Pescara,   5
    Under whom you hold certain land in cheat,
    Much 'gainst his noble nature hath been moved
    To seize those lands, and some of his dependants
    Are at this instant making it their suit
    To be invested in your revenues.   10
    I cannot think they mean well to your life
    That do deprive you of your means of life,
    Your living.
Antonio.   You are still an heretic
    To any safety I can shape myself.

Enter PESCARA.

Delio. Here comes the Marquis. I will make myself   15
    Petitioner for some part of your land,
    To know whither it is flying.
Antonio.   I pray, do.   [*He retires.*]

    V.i.0.1.] located in Milan, in a secluded street or public place near the
palace.
    2. *misdoubt*] distrust, am suspicious of.
    4. *repair*] return.
    6. *in cheat*] 'subject to escheat'; Antonio possessed land on condition that
if he died intestate without heirs, or if he committed treason, felony, etc., it
would revert to Pescara.

Delio. Sir, I have a suit to you.

Pescara.   To me?

Delio.   An easy one:

 There is the Citadel of Saint Bennet,

 With some demesnes, of late in the possession   20

 Of Antonio Bologna—please you bestow them on me?

Pescara. You are my friend, but this is such a suit

 Nor fit for me to give nor you to take.

Delio. No, sir?

Pescara.   I will give you ample reason for 't

 Soon in private.

Enter JULIA.

      Here's the Cardinal's mistress.   25

Julia. My lord, I am grown your poor petitioner,

 And should be an ill beggar, had I not

 A great man's letter here, the Cardinal's,

 To court you in my favour.   *[Gives letter.]*

Pescara. [*After reading*]   He entreats for you

 The Citadel of Saint Bennet, that belonged   30

 To the banished Bologna.

Julia.   Yes.

Pescara. I could not have thought of a friend I could

 Rather pleasure with it. 'Tis yours.

Julia.   Sir, I thank you;

 And he shall know how doubly I am engaged

 Both in your gift and speediness of giving,   35

 Which makes your grant the greater.   *Exit.*

Antonio. [*Aside*]   How they fortify

 Themselves with my ruin!

Delio.   Sir, I am

 Little bound to you.

Pescara.   Why?

Delio. Because you denied this suit to me, and gave 't

 To such a creature.

Pescara.   Do you know what it was?   40

 It was Antonio's land: not forfeited

 By course of law, but ravished from his throat

---

19. *Bennet*] Benedict.

By the Cardinal's entreaty. It were not fit
I should bestow so main a piece of wrong
Upon my friend; 'tis a gratification   45
Only due to a strumpet, for it is injustice.
Shall I sprinkle the pure blood of innocents
To make those followers I call my friends
Look ruddier upon me? I am glad
This land, ta'en from the owner by such wrong,   50
Returns again unto so foul an use
As salary for his lust. Learn, good Delio,
To ask noble things of me, and you shall find
I'll be a noble giver.
Delio.   You instruct me well.
Antonio. [*Aside*] Why, here's a man now would fright
        impudence   55
    From sauciest beggars.
Pescara. Prince Ferdinand's come to Milan
    Sick, as they give out, of an apoplexy;
    But some say 'tis a frenzy. I am going
    To visit him.   *Exit.*
Antonio.   'Tis a noble old fellow.   [*He advances.*]   60
Delio. What course do you mean to take, Antonio?
Antonio. This night I mean to venture all my fortune,
    Which is no more than a poor ling'ring life,
    To the Cardinal's worst of malice. I have got
    Private access to his chamber, and intend   65
    To visit him, about the mid of night,
    As once his brother did our noble Duchess.

---

44. *so main . . . wrong*] so great a portion of what has been wrongfully obtained.

49. *ruddier*] i.e. more favourably.

55–6.] i.e. why, this Pescara would know how to refuse the most persistent beggars.

58. *as . . . out*] as people say.

apoplexy] sudden violent fit.

59. *frenzy*] considered an inflammation of the brain due to an invasion of choler; an advanced, delirious form of madness, in which speech becomes incomprehensible.

60. *'Tis . . . fellow*] Antonio now gives an ironic twist to Delio's earlier judgement (l. 7).

64. *malice*] power to harm (as well as 'ill will').

                    It may be that the sudden apprehension
                    Of danger—for I'll go in mine own shape—
                    When he shall see it fraught with love and duty,   70
                    May draw the poison out of him and work
                    A friendly reconcilement. If it fail,
                    Yet it shall rid me of this infamous calling;
                    For better fall once than be ever falling.
Delio. I'll second you in all danger; and, how e'er,   75
                    My life keeps rank with yours.
Antonio. You are still my loved and best friend.   *Exeunt.*

Scene ii

                              Enter PESCARA *and a* Doctor.

Pescara. Now, doctor, may I visit your patient?
Doctor. If 't please your lordship. But he's instantly
                    To take the air here in the gallery,
                    By my direction.
Pescara.   Pray thee, what's his disease?
Doctor. A very pestilent disease, my lord,   5
                    They call lycanthropia. (turning into a werewolf)
Pescara.   What's that?
                    I need a dictionary to 't.
Doctor.   I'll tell you.
                    In those that are possessed with 't there o'erflows
                    Such melancholy humour they imagine
                    Themselves to be transformèd into wolves,   10
                    Steal forth to churchyards in the dead of night,
                    And dig dead bodies up; as two nights since
                    One met the Duke, 'bout midnight in a lane
                    Behind Saint Mark's Church, with the leg of a man

---

70. *fraught with*] filled with, accompanied by.
73. *calling*] position in life, means of livelihood.
75. *how e'er*] whatever happens.

V.ii.o.1.] in a palace in Milan.
3–4. *To take . . . direction*] Doctors recommended that melancholic patients should expose themselves only to warm, moist air, and take only moderate exercise.
gallery] long room in which to take exercise indoors.

Upon his shoulder; and he howled fearfully;   15
Said he was a wolf, only the difference
Was, a wolf's skin was hairy on the outside,
His on the inside; bade them take their swords,
Rip up his flesh, and try. Straight I was sent for,
And, having ministered to him, found his grace   20
Very well recovered.

Pescara.   I am glad on 't.

Doctor. Yet not without some fear
Of a relapse. If he grow to his fit again,
I'll go a nearer way to work with him
Than ever Paracelsus dreamed of: if   25
They'll give me leave, I'll buffet his madness out of him.

Enter FERDINAND, MALATESTE, *and* Cardinal; BOSOLA
[*follows and watches, apart*].

Stand aside; he comes.

Ferdinand. Leave me.

Malateste. Why doth your lordship love this solitariness?

Ferdinand. Eagles commonly fly alone; they are crows, daws,   30
and starlings that flock together.—Look, what's that follows me?

Malateste. Nothing, my lord.

Ferdinand. Yes.

Malateste. 'Tis your shadow.   35

Ferdinand. Stay it; let it not haunt me.

Malateste. Impossible, if you move and the sun shine.

Ferdinand. I will throttle it.

[*Throws himself down on his shadow.*]

Malateste. O, my lord, you are angry with nothing.

Ferdinand. You are a fool: how is 't possible I should catch   40

---

24. *nearer*] more direct, quicker; or, possibly, 'more intimate, familiar'.

25. *Paracelsus*] a famed physician-magician (1493–1541).

26. *buffet*] Whipping was a recommended and usual remedy, as well as a means of controlling madmen.

28–9.] Pleasant company was recommended as a cure for those suffering from melancholy; *solitariness* was forbidden.

30. *daws*] jackdaws.

31–41. *Look . . . upon 't*] 'To be afraid of one's own shadow' was a prover-bial expression for causeless fear, and 'to fight with one's own shadow' for a vain or useless act.

my shadow unless I fall upon 't? When I go to hell, I
mean to carry a bribe; for look you, good gifts evermore
make way for the worst persons.

Pescara. Rise, good my lord.

Ferdinand. I am studying the art of patience.   45

Pescara. 'Tis a noble virtue.

Ferdinand. To drive six snails before me, from this town to
Moscow; neither use goad nor whip to them, but let them
take their own time—the patientest man i'th' world
match me for an experiment!—and I'll crawl after like a   50
sheep-biter.

Cardinal. Force him up.   [*They raise him.*]

Ferdinand. Use me well, you were best. What I have done, I
have done; I'll confess nothing.

Doctor. Now let me come to him.—Are you mad, my lord?   55
Are you out of your princely wits?

Ferdinand. What's he?

Pescara. Your doctor.

Ferdinand. Let me have his beard sawed off, and his eyebrows
filed more civil.   60

Doctor. I must do mad tricks with him, for that's the only way
on 't.—I have brought your grace a salamander's skin, to
keep you from sunburning.

Ferdinand. I have cruel sore eyes.

Doctor. The white of a cockatrix's egg is present remedy.   65

42–3. *good . . . persons*] alluding to the practice of bribing gaolers in public
prisons of the time.

45–6.] Cf. the common dictum: 'Patience is a virtue'.

51. *sheep-biter*] dog that worries sheep.

53–4. *What . . . done*] The more common proverb was 'I know what I
know'. Possibly there is an echo here of Shakespeare's modifications: see
Lady Macbeth's 'What's done is done' (*Macbeth*, III.ii.7) or Iago's 'What you
know, you know. / From this time forth I never will speak word' (*Othello*,
V.ii.306–7).

60. *civil*] decent, becoming.

61. *mad tricks*] another recommended cure for madness, but of disputed
worth.

62. *salamander's skin*] The skin of this lizard-like creature was supposed to
resist fire, as the *salamander* itself was said to live in it and be able to quench
it.

65.] Isaiah, the Old Testament prophet, wrote of this imaginary creature
that wicked and violent men 'hatch cockatrice's eggs' and also that 'he that
eateth of their eggs will die' (Isaiah, 59.4–8).

present] instant, immediate.

Ferdinand. Let it be a new-laid one, you were best.—
    Hide me from him! Physicians are like kings,
    They brook no contradiction.
Doctor. Now he begins to fear me; now let me alone with him.
Cardinal. How now, put off your gown?   70
Doctor. Let me have some forty urinals filled with rose-water;
    he and I'll go pelt one another with them.—Now he
    begins to fear me.—Can you fetch a frisk, sir?—Let him
    go, let him go, upon my peril: I find by his eye he stands
    in awe of me. I'll make him as tame as a dormouse.   75
Ferdinand. Can you fetch your frisks, sir?—I will stamp him
    into a cullis, flay off his skin, to cover one of the anato-
    mies this rogue hath set i'th' cold yonder, in Barber-
    Chirurgeons' Hall.—Hence, hence! You are all of you
    like beasts for sacrifice; there's nothing left of you but   80
    tongue and belly, flattery and lechery.   [*Exit.*]
Pescara. Doctor, he did not fear you throughly.
Doctor. True, I was somewhat too forward.   [*Exit.*]
Bosola. Mercy upon me, what a fatal judgement
    Hath fall'n upon this Ferdinand!
Pescara.   Knows your grace   85
    What accident hath brought unto the prince
    This strange distraction?
Cardinal. [*Aside*] I must feign somewhat. [*To them*] Thus they
    say it grew:

---

    68. *brook*] tolerate.
    69. *let . . . him*] leave him to me.
    70. *put . . . gown*] in preparation for more violent treatments.
    73. *fetch a frisk*] cut a caper.
    75. *dormouse*] i.e. a tiny hibernating animal.
    76. *stamp*] pound, crush, as in a mortar; trample.
    77. *cullis*] broth (often made from pulverized ingredients).
    77–9. *one . . . Hall*] Dead bodies, especially of executed criminals, were
brought to the Barber-Surgeons' (*Chirurgeons'*) Hall, in Monkswell Street,
near Cripplegate, London, where they were either dissected or preserved and
displayed as specimens (*anatomies*) in its museum.
    81. *tongue and belly*] In ancient sacrifices the tongue and entrails were left
for the gods. Here they represent flattery and appetite.
    82. *throughly*] thoroughly.
    86. *accident*] circumstance.
    87. *distraction*] madness.

You have heard it rumoured for these many years,
None of our family dies but there is seen   90
The shape of an old woman, which is given
By tradition to us to have been murdered
By her nephews, for her riches; such a figure
One night, as the prince sat up late at 's book,
Appeared to him; when, crying out for help,   95
The gentlemen of 's chamber found his grace
All on a cold sweat, altered much in face
And language. Since which apparition,
He hath grown worse and worse, and I much fear
He cannot live.   100
Bosola. Sir, I would speak with you.
Pescara.   We'll leave your grace,
Wishing to the sick prince, our noble lord,
All health of mind and body.
Cardinal.   You are most welcome.
              [*Exeunt all except* Cardinal *and* BOSOLA.]
[*Aside*] Are you come? So.—This fellow must not know
By any means I had intelligence   105
In our Duchess' death; for, though I counselled it,
The full of all th' engagement seemed to grow
From Ferdinand. [*To Bosola*] Now, sir, how fares our
    sister?
I do not think but sorrow makes her look
Like to an oft-dyed garment: she shall now   110
Taste comfort from me.—Why do you look so wildly?
O, the fortune of your master here, the prince,
Dejects you, but be you of happy comfort:

---

90. *but*] except.
91. *shape*] used of both spectral and imaginary appearances.
    given] presented, interpreted.
99–100. *I . . . live*] By inventing a 'tradition' that implies that his brother is
incurable, the Cardinal tries to frighten off his hearers and prevent any
attempt to help his brother. He may also be preparing them for a death that
he is thinking of bringing about himself (he had been the one to 'counsel' his
sister's death, see ll. 105–7, below. Bosola sees death in his eyes (see ll. 145–
6, below) and the Cardinal has reason for murder now (see ll. 224–6, below).
Julia will soon be another victim, the Cardinal being ready to take advantage
of a situation he could not have foreseen (see ll. 227–9).

If you'll do one thing for me I'll entreat,
Though he had a cold tombstone o'er his bones,   115
I'd make you what you would be.
Bosola.   Any thing—
Give it me in a breath, and let me fly to 't:
They that think long, small expedition win,
For, musing much o'th' end, cannot begin.

Enter JULIA.

Julia. Sir, will you come in to supper?
Cardinal.   I am busy; leave me.   120
Julia. [*Aside*] What an excellent shape hath that fellow!
                                              Exit.
Cardinal. 'Tis thus: Antonio lurks here in Milan;
Inquire him out, and kill him. While he lives,
Our sister cannot marry, and I have thought
Of an excellent match for her. Do this, and style me   125
Thy advancement.
Bosola. But by what means shall I find him out?
Cardinal. There is a gentleman called Delio
Here in the camp, that hath been long approved
His loyal friend. Set eye upon that fellow,   130
Follow him to mass—may be Antonio,
Although he do account religion
But a school-name, for fashion of the world
May accompany him; or else go inquire out

115–16. *Though . . . be*] i.e. even if (as a consequence) my brother were
dead, I would ensure you became whatever you wished to be.

117. *Give . . . to 't*] i.e. tell me in a word and I am very ready to act.
Perhaps Bosola answers with wordplay on *breath* = 'power of breathing, life';
hence 'Bring your sister back to life and I am completely content'—a secret
meaning, for his own satisfaction.

118. *small expedition win*] make little progress.

119.] since deliberating excessively on the outcome makes one unable to
begin.

125–6. *style . . . advancement*] name the office you would like to claim as
your reward.

129. *camp*] military encampment. The Cardinal is still involved as a 'soldier' in the preparations started at III.iii.1.

approved] shown to be; esteemed.

133. *But a school-name*] a mere invention of the Church Fathers.

Delio's confessor, and see if you can bribe   135
Him to reveal it. There are a thousand ways
A man might find to trace him: as to know
What fellows haunt the Jews for taking up
Great sums of money, for sure he's in want;
Or else to go to th' picture-makers and learn   140
Who bought her picture lately. Some of these
Happily may take—

Bosola.   Well, I'll not freeze i'th' business;
I would see that wretched thing, Antonio,
Above all sights i'th' world.

Cardinal.   Do, and be happy.   *Exit.*

Bosola. This fellow doth breed basilisks in 's eyes;   145
He's nothing else but murder: yet he seems
Not to have notice of the Duchess' death.—
'Tis his cunning. I must follow his example;
There cannot be a surer way to trace
Than that of an old fox.

[*Enter* JULIA, *pointing a pistol at him.*]

Julia.   So, sir, you are well met.   150

Bosola. How now?

Julia.   Nay, the doors are fast enough.—
Now sir, I will make you confess your treachery.

Bosola. Treachery?

Julia.   Yes, confess to me
Which of my women 'twas you hired to put
Love-powder into my drink?

Bosola.   Love-powder!

Julia.   Yes,   155
When I was at Malfi.—

---

138. *haunt the Jews*] frequent usurers.
  taking up] borrowing.
  141. *bought*] suggesting that Antonio will need some substitute for the presence of his wife (as Isabella, in *W.D.*, kisses her absent husband's picture every night before bed; II.ii.25–8).
  143–4. *I . . . i'th' world*] Bosola answers in words that secretly suggest his own total commitment to the Duchess's cause; see, for example, IV.ii.338–40.
  144. *happy*] fortunate, successful.
  145. *basilisks*] See III.ii.87 and note.

Why should I fall in love with such a face else?
I have already suffered for thee so much pain,
The only remedy to do me good
Is to kill my longing.
Bosola.   Sure your pistol holds   160
Nothing but perfumes, or kissing-comfits.
Excellent lady,
You have a pretty way on 't to discover
Your longing. Come, come, I'll disarm you,
And arm you thus.—Yet this is wondrous strange.   165
Julia. Compare thy form and my eyes together,
You'll find my love no such great miracle.
Now you'll say
I am wanton.—This nice modesty in ladies
Is but a troublesome familiar   170
That haunts them.
Bosola. Know you me; I am a blunt soldier.
Julia.   The better—
Sure, there wants fire where there are no lively sparks
Of roughness.
Bosola.   And I want compliment.
Julia.   Why, ignorance
In courtship cannot make you do amiss,   175
If you have a heart to do well.
Bosola.   You are very fair.
Julia. Nay, if you lay beauty to my charge,
I must plead unguilty.
Bosola.   Your bright eyes
Carry a quiver of darts in them, sharper

---

161. *kissing-comfits*] sweetmeats to perfume the breath.

163. *discover*] uncover, show.

165. *arm*] embrace.

166. *form*] shape, body (cf. l. 121, above).

169. *nice*] shy, fastidious, reluctant, trivial.

170. *familiar*] familiar spirit. See I.i.259, note.

172–3. *Sure . . . roughness*] i.e. Surely, there is little passion without some aggression (a lack of good manners).

174. *want compliment*] lack good social manners, courtesy.

178–80. *Your . . . sunbeams*] Bosola neatly uses two commonplaces of courtship in one prompt response.

Than sunbeams.

Julia.   You will mar me with commendation;   180
Put yourself to the charge of courting me,
Whereas now I woo you.

Bosola. [*Aside*] I have it; I will work upon this creature.
[*To her*] Let us grow most amorously familiar.
If the great Cardinal now should see me thus,   185
Would he not count me a villain?

Julia. No, he might count me a wanton,
Not lay a scruple of offence on you;
For if I see and steal a diamond,
The fault is not i'th' stone but in me the thief   190
That purloins it.—I am sudden with you;
We that are great women of pleasure use to cut off
These uncertain wishes and unquiet longings,
And in an instant join the sweet delight
And the pretty excuse together. Had you been i'th'
       street,   195
Under my chamber window, even there
I should have courted you.

Bosola.   O, you are an excellent lady.

Julia. Bid me do somewhat for you presently,
To express I love you.

Bosola.   I will, and if you love me
Fail not to effect it.   200
The Cardinal is grown wondrous melancholy;
Demand the cause. Let him not put you off
With feigned excuse; discover the main ground on 't.

Julia. Why would you know this?

Bosola.   I have depended on him,
And I hear that he is fall'n in some disgrace   205
With the Emperor.—If he be, like the mice
That forsake falling houses, I would shift
To other dependence.

181.] Take it upon yourself to woo me.

188. *scruple*] minute quantity.

192. *use*] make it our practice.

198. *presently*] immediately.

206–7. *mice . . . houses*] so Pliny's *Natural History* and other ancient authorities; the saying was proverbial.

Julia. You shall not need follow the wars;
    I'll be your maintenance.
Bosola.   And I your loyal servant;   210
    But I cannot leave my calling.
Julia.   Not leave
    An ungrateful general for the love of a sweet lady?
    You are like some cannot sleep in feather beds,
    But must have blocks for their pillows.
Bosola.   Will you do this?
Julia. Cunningly.
Bosola.   Tomorrow I'll expect th' intelligence.   215
Julia. Tomorrow? Get you into my cabinet;
    You shall have it with you. Do not delay me,
    No more than I do you; I am like one
    That is condemned—I have my pardon promised,
    But I would see it sealed.—Go, get you in;   220
    You shall see me wind my tongue about his heart
    Like a skein of silk.   [*Exit* BOSOLA.]

        [*Enter* Cardinal, *followed by* Servants.]

Cardinal. Where are you?
Servant.   Here.
Cardinal.   Let none, upon your lives,
    Have conference with the Prince Ferdinand,
    Unless I know it.   [*Exeunt* Servants.]
            [*Aside*] In this distraction   225
    He may reveal the murder.
    Yon's my ling'ring consumption:
    I am weary of her, and by any means
    Would be quit of.
Julia.   How now, my lord?
    What ails you?
Cardinal.   Nothing.
Julia.   O, you are much altered.   230
    Come, I must be your secretary, and remove

---

213. *some*] some who.
217. *have it with you*] take it along with you when you leave.
220. *sealed*] signed and sealed.
229. *quit of*] rid of.
231. *secretary*] confidant.

This lead from off your bosom. What's the matter?

Cardinal. I may not tell you.

Julia. Are you so far in love with sorrow
    You cannot part with part of it? Or think you   235
    I cannot love your grace when you are sad
    As well as merry? Or do you suspect
    I, that have been a secret to your heart
    These many winters, cannot be the same
    Unto your tongue?

Cardinal.   Satisfy thy longing—   240
    The only way to make thee keep my counsel
    Is not to tell thee.

Julia.   Tell your echo this,
    Or flatterers, that like echoes still report
    What they hear though most imperfect, and not me;
    For, if that you be true unto yourself,   245
    I'll know.

Cardinal.   Will you rack me?

Julia.   No, judgement shall
    Draw it from you. It is an equal fault
    To tell one's secrets unto all or none.

Cardinal. The first argues folly.

Julia.   But the last, tyranny.

Cardinal. Very well. Why, imagine I have committed   250
    Some secret deed which I desire the world
    May never hear of.

Julia.   Therefore may not I know it?
    You have concealed for me as great a sin
    As adultery. Sir, never was occasion
    For perfect trial of my constancy   255
    Till now. Sir, I beseech you.

Cardinal.   You'll repent it.

Julia.   Never.

Cardinal. It hurries thee to ruin: I'll not tell thee.

241–2. *The . . . thee*] a proverbial slur on women; see IV.ii.225–6 and note.

245. *if . . . yourself*] i.e. if you'll keep faith with me, your 'other self'.

246. *rack*] torture on the rack to obtain a confession.

249. *the last, tyranny*] telling one's secrets to no one argues a bullying nature.

Be well advised, and think what danger 'tis
To receive a prince's secrets: they that do
Had need have their breasts hooped with adamant   260
To contain them. I pray thee, yet be satisfied,
Examine thine own frailty; 'tis more easy
To tie knots than unloose them. 'Tis a secret
That, like a ling'ring poison, may chance lie
Spread in thy veins, and kill thee seven year hence.   265

Julia. Now you dally with me.

Cardinal.   No more; thou shalt know it.
By my appointment, the great Duchess of Malfi,
And two of her young children, four nights since,
Were strangled.

Julia.   O heaven! Sir, what have you done?

Cardinal. How now? How settles this? Think you your bosom   270
Will be a grave, dark and obscure enough
For such a secret?

Julia.   You have undone yourself, sir.

Cardinal. Why?

Julia.   It lies not in me to conceal it.

Cardinal.   No?
Come, I will swear you to 't upon this book.

Julia. Most religiously.

Cardinal.   Kiss it.   [*She kisses the book.*]   275
Now you shall never utter it; thy curiosity
Hath undone thee: thou'rt poisoned with that book.
Because I knew thou couldst not keep my counsel,
I have bound thee to 't by death.

[*Enter* BOSOLA.]

Bosola. For pity sake, hold!

Cardinal.   Ha, Bosola!

Julia.   I forgive you   280

---

260. *adamant*] loadstone, diamond; the hardest iron or steel.

264–5. *may . . . veins*] may happen to linger in a dormant state in your blood.

270. *settles*] either 'sinks deeply' (i.e. into the mind) or 'settles down, becomes still and clear'. (An image from the settling of a liquid.)

273. *It lies . . . me*] I am unable.

280–1. *I . . . done*] i.e. I forgive your killing me in a way that justly repays what I have done to you—telling Bosola your secret.

> This equal piece of justice you have done,
> For I betrayed your counsel to that fellow.
> He overheard it; that was the cause I said
> It lay not in me to conceal it.

Bosola.   O foolish woman,   285
> Couldst not thou have poisoned him?

Julia.   'Tis weakness
> Too much to think what should have been done.—I go,
> I know not whither.   [*Dies.*]

Cardinal. [*To Bosola*]   Wherefore com'st thou hither?

Bosola. That I might find a great man, like yourself,
> Not out of his wits, as the Lord Ferdinand,   290
> To remember my service.

Cardinal.   I'll have thee hewed in pieces.

Bosola. Make not yourself such a promise of that life
> Which is not yours to dispose of.

Cardinal.   Who placed thee here?

Bosola. Her lust, as she intended.

Cardinal.   Very well;
> Now you know me for your fellow murderer.   295

Bosola. And wherefore should you lay fair marble colours
> Upon your rotten purposes to me,
> Unless you imitate some that do plot great treasons,
> And, when they have done, go hide themselves i'th'
>   graves
> Of those were actors in 't?   300

Cardinal. No more; there is a fortune attends thee.

Bosola. Shall I go sue to Fortune any longer?

287–8. *I . . . whither*] Devotional books and sermons often applied this phrase to death as a journey to an unknown destination; Webster had used it in *W.D.*, V.vi.107 (for Flamineo's parody of a dying speech) and 249 (for Vittoria's penultimate speech).

291. *remember*] remunerate.

292–3. *Make . . . of*] i.e. Don't boast of being able to kill someone whom you can't easily get rid of.

296–7.] i.e. And why should you put on a false face to your corrupt purposes, like painting rotten wood to look like marble?

298. *treasons*] acts of treason, betrayal.

299–300.] and, when their villainous work is done, conceal their own involvement by killing the agents who did their dirty work? (Bosola suspects that the Cardinal plans to get rid of him.)

'Tis the fool's pilgrimage.
Cardinal.   I have honours in store for thee.
Bosola. There are a many ways that conduct to seeming
    Honour, and some of them very dirty ones.   305
Cardinal. Throw to the devil
    Thy melancholy: the fire burns well;
    What need we keep a-stirring of 't, and make
    A greater smother? Thou wilt kill Antonio?
Bosola. Yes.
Cardinal.   Take up that body.
Bosola.   I think I shall   310
    Shortly grow the common bier for churchyards.
Cardinal. I will allow thee some dozen of attendants
    To aid thee in the murder.
Bosola.   O, by no means:
    Physicians that apply horse-leeches to any rank swelling
    use to cut off their tails, that the blood may run through   315
    them the faster. Let me have no train when I go to shed
    blood, lest it make me have a greater when I ride to the
    gallows.
Cardinal. Come to me after midnight, to help to remove that
    body to her own lodging. I'll give out she died o'th'   320
    plague; 'twill breed the less inquiry after her death.
Bosola. Where's Castruchio, her husband?
Cardinal. He's rode to Naples to take possession
    Of Antonio's citadel.
Bosola. Believe me, you have done a very happy turn.   325
Cardinal. Fail not to come. There is the master key
    Of our lodgings; and by that you may conceive
    What trust I plant in you.
Bosola.   You shall find me ready.
                                        Exit Cardinal.

---

303. *'Tis . . . pilgrimage*] i.e. One who seeks Fortune's favour is a fool.
304. *conduct*] lead.
309. *smother*] smoke that is dense and stifling.
310–11. *I . . . churchyards*] i.e. I'm on my way to becoming a wholesale
carrier of corpses.
314. *horse-leeches*] used to suck out the infected blood; cf. I.i.52–3.
316–18. *Let . . . gallows*] (Bosola wants no helpers, to lessen his chances of
being caught.)
325. *happy turn*] act of good will, with possible wordplay on *turn* = 'trick'.

O poor Antonio, though nothing be so needful
To thy estate as pity, yet I find   330
Nothing so dangerous! I must look to my footing;
In such slippery ice-pavements, men had need
To be frost-nailed well; they may break their necks else.
The precedent's here afore me: how this man
Bears up in blood! Seems fearless! Why, 'tis well: 335
Security some men call the suburbs of hell,
Only a dead wall between. Well, good Antonio,
I'll seek thee out, and all my care shall be
To put thee into safety from the reach
Of these most cruel biters, that have got   340
Some of thy blood already. It may be
I'll join with thee in a most just revenge.
The weakest arm is strong enough that strikes
With the sword of justice.—Still methinks the Duchess
Haunts me. There, there!—   345
'Tis nothing but my melancholy.
O Penitence, let me truly taste thy cup,
That throws men down only to raise them up!   *Exit.*

---

330. *estate*] condition, fortune.

333. *frost-nailed*] provided with hob-nailed boots for manoeuvring on ice.

335. *Bears . . . blood*] acts according to his breeding, in a bloody cause.
The phrase *in blood* is also a technical hunting-term, meaning 'full of life'.

336. *Security*] confidence that one is secure.

suburbs of hell] a common phrase among preachers.

337. *dead*] unbroken, continuous, common. The same sense is implied at
V.v.97, with a similar quibble by association with 'graves'.

340. *biters*] blood-suckers.

341. *thy blood*] i.e. your children.

345–6.] Perhaps a stage direction should be added to indicate that the
Duchess enters; in *W.D.*, IV.i.102, '*Enter Isabella's Ghost*' accompanies Francisco's '. . . I'll close mine eyes, / And in a melancholic thought I'll frame /
Her figure 'fore me . . . Methinks she stands afore me . . . 'Tis my melancholy.' Certainly Bosola should act as if he actually sees her, even if the
audience does not.

melancholy] A melancholic person may imagine 'a thousand chimeras and
visions, which to his thinking he certainly sees, bugbears, talks with black
men, ghosts, goblins, etc.' (Burton, *Anatomy of Melancholy*). Bosola's *melancholy* is now a true one, brought on by remorse, not the affectation of a
malcontent (cf. I.i.75, note).

347. *taste thy cup*] accept the bitter experience which you offer (a sense
derived from the New Testament's accounts of Jesus before his crucifixion).

Scene iii

Enter ANTONIO and DELIO.
[There is an] ECHO from the Duchess' grave.

Delio. Yon's the Cardinal's window. This fortification
 Grew from the ruins of an ancient abbey;
 And to yon side o'th' river lies a wall,
 Piece of a cloister, which in my opinion
 Gives the best echo that you ever heard,   5
 So hollow and so dismal, and withal
 So plain in the distinction of our words,
 That many have supposed it is a spirit
 That answers.
Antonio.   I do love these ancient ruins:
 We never tread upon them but we set   10
 Our foot upon some reverend history;
 And questionless, here in this open court,
 Which now lies naked to the injuries
 Of stormy weather, some men lie interred
 Loved the church so well, and gave so largely to 't,   15
 They thought it should have canopied their bones
 Till doomsday. But all things have their end;
 Churches and cities, which have diseases like to men,
 Must have like death that we have.
Echo.   *Like death that we have.*

V.iii.o.1.] See Introduction for the source and handling of this scene (pp. 24–5); its location, being unusual and unexpected, is identified at once in the opening speeches. Like III.iv (see note), this entire scene can be omitted in performance without detriment to the play's narrative; but the change of tone and tempo it effects, its presentation of the Duchess, as well as Antonio, and the dramatic effect of its echo all argue for its retention—and most modern productions do stage it.

4. *Piece of a cloister*] If a large stage property represents the Duchess's grave (see 0.2 S.D.), it might be revealed within an opening in the façade which backed the stage, its other entrance-ways and pillars representing the *cloister*. Antonio and Delio would then be standing as far as possible from it, near the front edge of the stage.

6. *dismal*] foreboding.

11. *reverend*] venerable.

15. *Loved*] who loved.

18. *diseases*] disturbances (as well as in the modern medical sense).

Delio. Now the echo hath caught you.

Antonio.　　　　　　　　It groaned, methought, and gave　20
　　A very deadly accent.

Echo.　　　　　　*Deadly accent.*

Delio. I told you 'twas a pretty one. You may make it
　　A huntsman, or a falconer, a musician,
　　Or a thing of sorrow.

Echo.　　　　　　*A thing of sorrow.*

Antonio. Ay, sure: that suits it best.

Echo.　　　　　　　　*That suits it best.*　25

Antonio. 'Tis very like my wife's voice.

Echo.　　　　　　　　*Ay, wife's voice.*

Delio. Come, let's walk farther from 't.
　　I would not have you go to th' Cardinal's tonight.
　　Do not.

Echo.　　*Do not.*

Delio. Wisdom doth not more moderate wasting sorrow　30
　　Than time: take time for 't; be mindful of thy safety.

Echo. Be mindful of thy safety.

Antonio.　　　　　　Necessity compels me:
　　Make scrutiny throughout the passes
　　Of your own life, you'll find it impossible
　　To fly your fate.

Echo.　　　　*O, fly your fate!*　35

Delio. Hark! The dead stones seem to have pity on you
　　And give you good counsel.

Antonio. Echo, I will not talk with thee,
　　For thou art a dead thing.

Echo.　　　　　　*Thou art a dead thing.*

Antonio. My Duchess is asleep now,　40
　　And her little ones, I hope sweetly. O heaven,
　　Shall I never see her more?

---

27. *let's*] an emendation of Q's 'let's vs'.

30–1. *Wisdom . . . time*] Time does more than human wisdom can to ease the anguish of debilitating sorrow.

33. *passes*] events.

41. *heaven*] another occasion when Webster may have written 'God' and censorship required a change.

42–5.] Here, as at V.ii.345–6, the Duchess may return to the stage, perhaps appearing within a grave that now opens (see Introduction, pp. 24–5).

Echo.   *Never see her more.*
Antonio. I marked not one repetition of the echo
    But that; and on the sudden, a clear light
    Presented me a face folded in sorrow.   45
Delio. Your fancy, merely.
Antonio. Come, I'll be out of this ague,
    For to live thus is not indeed to live;
    It is a mockery and abuse of life.
    I will not henceforth save myself by halves;   50
    Lose all, or nothing.
Delio.   Your own virtue save you!
    I'll fetch your eldest son, and second you.
    It may be that the sight of his own blood
    Spread in so sweet a figure may beget
    The more compassion.
Antonio.   How ever, fare you well.   55
    Though in our miseries Fortune have a part,
    Yet in our noble suff'rings she hath none;
    Contempt of pain, that we may call our own.   *Exeunt.*

Scene iv

    Enter Cardinal, PESCARA, MALATESTE, RODERIGO,
                and GRISOLAN.

Cardinal. You shall not watch tonight by the sick prince;
    His grace is very well recovered.

---

44. *a clear light*] As the following scene is to be 'after midnight' (V.ii.319),
this one may also be played as in darkness, with Antonio and Delio signifying
this by holding torches. Perhaps an actual darkening of the stage and auditorium increased the eerie atmosphere of this scene among ruins; the indoors
auditorium of the Blackfriars could be darkened at any time of year, while at
the open-air Globe Theatre evening would begin to set in during winter
months well before the end of the play. In these conditions, an actual *light*
from the grave would shine more *clearly*.

45. *folded*] enveloped or, perhaps, bent down.

47. *ague*] fever; and see V.iv.67–9.

53. *his*] i.e. the Cardinal's.

54. *Spread*] (1) displayed; (2) disseminated.

V.iv.0.1.] Located in the Cardinal's apartment; it is night-time and lights
are carried on stage.

Malateste. Good my lord, suffer us.

Cardinal.   O, by no means;
    The noise, and change of object in his eye,
    Doth more distract him. I pray, all to bed,   5
    And, though you hear him in his violent fit,
    Do not rise, I entreat you.

Pescara. So, sir, we shall not—

Cardinal.   Nay, I must have you promise
    Upon your honours, for I was enjoined to 't
    By himself, and he seemed to urge it sensibly.   10

Pescara. Let our honours bind this trifle.

Cardinal. Nor any of your followers.

Malateste.   Neither.

Cardinal. It may be to make trial of your promise,
    When he's asleep, myself will rise and feign
    Some of his mad tricks, and cry out for help,   15
    And feign myself in danger.

Malateste.   If your throat were cutting,
    I'd not come at you, now I have protested against it.

Cardinal. Why, I thank you.   [*Withdraws.*]

Grisolan.   'Twas a foul storm tonight.

Roderigo. The Lord Ferdinand's chamber shook like an osier.

Malateste. 'Twas nothing but pure kindness in the devil   20
    To rock his own child.   *Exeunt* [*all except the* Cardinal].

Cardinal. The reason why I would not suffer these
    About my brother is because at midnight
    I may with better privacy convey
    Julia's body to her own lodging.—   25
    O, my conscience!
    I would pray now, but the devil takes away my heart
    For having any confidence in prayer.
    About this hour I appointed Bosola
    To fetch the body: when he hath served my turn,   30
    He dies.   *Exit.*

Enter BOSOLA.

11.] Let us bind ourselves by oath to honour this small request.

17. *protested*] sworn an oath.

19. *osier*] wicker basket.

28. *For*] from.

Bosola. Hah? 'Twas the Cardinal's voice. I heard him name
    Bosola, and my death.—Listen; I hear one's footing.

Enter FERDINAND.

Ferdinand. Strangling is a very quiet death.
Bosola. [*Aside*] Nay then, I see I must stand upon my guard.   35
Ferdinand. What say' to that? Whisper, softly: Do you agree
    to 't?
    So, it must be done i'th' dark; the Cardinal
    Would not for a thousand pounds the doctor should see it.
Exit.

Bosola. My death is plotted; here's the consequence of
    murder.
    We value not desert, nor Christian breath,   40
    When we know black deeds must be cured with death.

Enter ANTONIO and Servant.

Servant. Here stay, sir, and be confident, I pray;
    I'll fetch you a dark lantern.   *Exit.*
Antonio. [*To himself*] Could I take him at his prayers,
    There were hope of pardon.
Bosola.   Fall right my sword!   45
[Stabs Antonio.]
    I'll not give thee so much leisure as to pray.
Antonio. O, I am gone! Thou hast ended a long suit
    In a minute.
Bosola.   What art thou?
Antonio.   A most wretched thing,
    That only have thy benefit in death,
    To appear myself.

[Enter Servant with a light.]

Servant.   Where are you, sir?   50

---

    36. *say'*] say you.
    41. black . . . death] a rehandling of a proverb Webster had used in *W.D.*,
II.i.319: 'Small mischiefs are by greater made secure'.
    43. *dark lantern*] Cf. II.iii.0.1 and note.
    47. *suit*] (1) petition (punning on 'pray' of the previous line); (2) quest,
chase.
    49. *benefit*] assistance, favour.
    50. *To . . . myself*] to be what I am, my mere self. A quibbling answer to
Bosola's 'What art thou?' (l. 48).

Antonio. Very near my home.—Bosola!

Servant.   O, misfortune!

Bosola. [*To Servant*] Smother thy pity; thou art dead else.—
    Antonio!
    The man I would have saved 'bove mine own life!
    We are merely the stars' tennis balls, struck and banded
    Which way please them.—O good Antonio,   55
    I'll whisper one thing in thy dying ear
    Shall make thy heart break quickly: Thy fair Duchess
    And two sweet children—

Antonio.   Their very names
    Kindle a little life in me.

Bosola.   Are murdered!

Antonio. Some men have wished to die   60
    At the hearing of sad tidings; I am glad
    That I shall do 't in sadness. I would not now
    Wish my wounds balmed, nor healed, for I have no use
    To put my life to. In all our quest of greatness,
    Like wanton boys whose pastime is their care,   65
    We follow after bubbles, blown in th' air.
    Pleasure of life, what is 't? Only the good hours
    Of an ague, merely a preparative to rest,
    To endure vexation.—I do not ask
    The process of my death; only commend me   70
    To Delio.

Bosola. Break, heart!

Antonio.   And let my son fly the courts of princes.
                               [*Dies.*]

Bosola. Thou seem'st to have loved Antonio?

Servant.   I brought him hither,
    To have reconciled him to the Cardinal.

Bosola. I do not ask thee that.   75

---

    51. *my home*] my last resting place, in death.

    54. *banded*] bandied.

    62. *in sadness*] in earnest; punning on *sad* of l. 61.

    68–9. *merely . . . vexation*] Cf. almost the last words of Flamineo, in *W.D.*,
V.vi.273–4: 'rest breeds rest, where all seek pain by pain'; also cf. *The
Duchess*, II.v.59–61.

    70. *process*] story.

    72. *And . . . princes*] Cf. the last words of Vittoria, in *W.D.*, V.vi.261–2: 'O
happy they that never saw the court, / Nor ever knew great man but by report'.

Take him up, if thou tender thine own life,
And bear him where the Lady Julia
Was wont to lodge.—O, my fate moves swift!
I have this Cardinal in the forge already;
Now I'll bring him to th' hammer.—O direful
　　misprision!　　　　　　　　　　　　　　　　80
I will not imitate things glorious,
No more than base; I'll be mine own example.
On, on; and look thou represent, for silence,
The thing thou bear'st.

　　　　　　Exeunt[,*the* Servant *bearing* ANTONIO'*s body*].

Scene v

　　　　　　Enter Cardinal, *with a book*.

Cardinal.　I am puzzled in a question about hell:
　　He says, in hell there's one material fire,
　　And yet it shall not burn all men alike.
　　Lay him by.—How tedious is a guilty conscience!
　　When I look into the fish ponds, in my garden,　　5
　　Methinks I see a thing, armed with a rake,
　　That seems to strike at me.—

　　　　　　Enter BOSOLA, *and* Servant *with* ANTONIO'S *body*.

　　　　　　　　　　　　Now! Art thou come?

---

76. *tender*] care for.
80. *misprision*] (1) concealment (of treason); (2) misapprehension, mistake.
81–2.] Cf. the words of the dying Flamineo, in *W.D.*, V.vi.256–7: 'I do not look / Who went before, nor who shall follow me'.
83–4. *and* . . . *bear'st*] and see to it that you say not a word about the death of him you bear off.

V.v.0.1.] The location appears to be the same as for the last scene, although at its close a more public place seems to be required, as Delio presents the new prince.
　with a book] a long-established stage-device for indicating melancholy or introspection; *Hamlet*, II.ii.166 is a famous example.
　4. *Lay him by*] put that author aside. The line is echoed later, at ll. 89–90.
　tedious] wearisome, painful, troublesome.
　7 S.D. Enter BOSOLA] The timing of this entry, on talk of striking, accentuates its menace and the sense of Fate moving swiftly and inexorably. The Cardinal appears not to see the dead Antonio until l. 37.

    Thou look'st ghastly;
    There sits in thy face some great determination,
    Mixed with some fear.

Bosola.   Thus it lightens into action: 10
    I am come to kill thee.

Cardinal.   Hah? Help! Our guard!

Bosola. Thou art deceived;
    They are out of thy howling.

Cardinal. Hold: and I will faithfully divide
    Revenues with thee.

Bosola.   Thy prayers and proffers   15
    Are both unseasonable.

Cardinal.   Raise the watch!
    We are betrayed!

Bosola.   I have confined your flight;
    I'll suffer your retreat to Julia's chamber,
    But no further.

Cardinal.   Help! We are betrayed!

        Enter[, above,] PESCARA, MALATESTE,
            RODERIGO[, *and* GRISOLAN].

Malateste.   Listen.

Cardinal. My dukedom for rescue!

Roderigo.   Fie upon his counterfeiting!   20

Malateste. Why, 'tis not the Cardinal.

Roderigo.   Yes, yes, 'tis he,
    But I'll see him hanged ere I'll go down to him.

Cardinal. Here's a plot upon me. I am assaulted! I am lost,
    Unless some rescue!

Grisolan.   He doth this pretty well,
    But it will not serve to laugh me out of mine honour.   25

Cardinal. The sword's at my throat!

Roderigo.   You would not bawl so loud then.

Malateste. Come, come,
    Let's go to bed; he told us thus much aforehand.

---

    8. *ghastly*] causing terror, ghost-like; full of fear, terrified.

    9. *sits*] is settled, fixed.

    determination] (1) resolution; (2) conclusion, end (a legal metaphor).

    10. *lightens*] ignites, flashes (as of lightning); with a pun on 'en*lighten*'.

    13. *howling*] for Webster, often implying wailing and tears (see *W.D.*,
V.iii.35–7; V.iv.56–65; V.vi.154–6).

    19 S.D. above] so Q4; see ll. 22 and 31.

Pescara. He wished you should not come at him; but, believe 't,
    The accent of the voice sounds not in jest.   30
    I'll down to him, howsoever, and with engines
    Force ope the doors.   *[Exit above.]*
Roderigo.   Let's follow him aloof,
    And note how the Cardinal will laugh at him.

              [Exeunt, above, MALATESTE, RODERIGO,
                       and GRISOLAN.]

Bosola. There's for you first,   *He kills the Servant.*
    'Cause you shall not unbarricade the door   35
    To let in rescue.
Cardinal. What cause hast thou to pursue my life?
Bosola.   Look there.
Cardinal. Antonio!
Bosola.   Slain by my hand unwittingly.—
    Pray, and be sudden. When thou killed'st thy sister,
    Thou took'st from Justice her most equal balance,   40
    And left her naught but her sword.
Cardinal.   O, mercy!
Bosola. Now it seems thy greatness was only outward;
    For thou fall'st faster of thyself than calamity
    Can drive thee. I'll not waste longer time. There!
                      [Stabs him.]
Cardinal. Thou hast hurt me.
Bosola.   Again!   *[Stabs him again.]*
Cardinal.   Shall I die like a leveret   45
    Without any resistance? Help, help, help!
    I am slain!

              Enter FERDINAND.

Ferdinand.   Th' alarum! Give me a fresh horse.
    Rally the vaunt-guard, or the day is lost.

---

   31. *engines*] implements, tools.
   42–4.] Unlike Ferdinand and Bosola, the Cardinal changes in a moment to a grovelling and panicking suppliant; see note l. 13, above. When he is wounded by his brother, however, he recognizes the demands of Justice (see l. 40) and regains control of himself (ll. 53–5, and following).
   45. *leveret*] young hare (too feeble and fearful to be worth hunting).
   47. *Give . . . horse*] Cf. the king's stirring cry in Shakespeare's *Richard III*, V.iv.7 and 13: 'My kingdom for a horse': a great contrast to the Cardinal's cry at l. 20, above.
   48. *vaunt-guard*] vanguard; the obsolete form is kept for its associations with *vaunt* = 'boast'.

Yield, yield! I give you the honour of arms,
Shake my sword over you.—Will you yield?   50
Cardinal. Help me; I am your brother.
Ferdinand.   The devil!
My brother fight upon the adverse party?
There flies your ransom.

> *He wounds the Cardinal, and in the*
> *scuffle gives Bosola his death wound.*

Cardinal.   O Justice!
I suffer now, for what hath former been:
Sorrow is held the eldest child of sin.   55
Ferdinand. Now you're brave fellows. Caesar's fortune was
harder than Pompey's; Caesar died in the arms of pros-
perity, Pompey at the feet of disgrace—you both died in
the field. The pain's nothing; pain many times is taken
away with the apprehension of greater, as the toothache   60
with the sight of a barber that comes to pull it out.—
There's philosophy for you.
Bosola. Now my revenge is perfect: *He kills Ferdinand.*
                            Sink, thou main cause
Of my undoing!—The last part of my life
Hath done me best service.   65
Ferdinand. Give me some wet hay; I am broken-winded.
I do account this world but a dog-kennel:
I will vault credit, and affect high pleasures

---

49. *I . . . arms*] i.e. I treat you as a soldier (giving the opportunity to surrender); cf. 'ransom' (l. 53, below).

53. *There . . . ransom*] i.e. being killed, you cannot be held for ransom.

55.] Giovanni's warning to Flamineo (*W.D.*, V.iv.21–3) spells out the religious implications: 'Study your prayers, sir, and be penitent. / 'Twere fit you'd think on what hath former been; / I have heard grief named the eldest child of sin.'

56. *brave*] splendid; courageous.

56–8. *Caesar's . . . disgrace*] Julius Caesar was assassinated in the Senate House at the height of his power; Pompey the Great, having been defeated in battle, was pursued, captured, and executed.

61. *barber*] Specialist dentists were not established until the mid-seventeenth century.

63 S.D.] Q has this direction at l. 65. The compositor probably placed it where he found a convenient space when he was setting these lines; he certainly misplaced the direction at IV.ii.236 for this reason.

kills] stabs fatally (allowing brief time still for speech).

66.] Grass in summer and wet hay in winter were recommended cures for a horse that was *broken-winded*.

68. *vault credit*] overleap expectation, reputation.
affect] aspire to.

Beyond death.

Bosola.   He seems to come to himself,
Now he's so near the bottom.   70

Ferdinand. My sister! O, my sister! There's the cause on 't:
Whether we fall by ambition, blood, or lust,
Like diamonds, we are cut with our own dust.   [*Dies.*]

Cardinal. Thou hast thy payment too.

Bosola. Yes, I hold my weary soul in my teeth;   75
'Tis ready to part from me.—I do glory
That thou, which stood'st like a huge pyramid
Begun upon a large and ample base,
Shalt end in a little point, a kind of nothing.

[*Enter* PESCARA, MALATESTE, RODERIGO, *and* GRISOLAN.]

Pescara. How now, my lord?

Malateste.   O, sad disaster!

Roderigo.   How comes this?   80

Bosola. Revenge, for the Duchess of Malfi, murdered
By th' Aragonian brethren; for Antonio,
Slain by this hand; for lustful Julia,
Poisoned by this man; and lastly for myself,
That was an actor in the main of all   85
Much 'gainst mine own good nature, yet i'th' end
Neglected.

Pescara. [*To Cardinal*] How now, my lord?

Cardinal.   Look to my brother.
He gave us these large wounds, as we were struggling
Here i'th' rushes.—And now, I pray, let me
Be laid by, and never thought of.   [*Dies.*]   90

---

69. *come to himself*] recover his wits.

70. *near the bottom*] near death. Perhaps a reference to the turning of Fortune's wheel, drawing him down (see 'come', l. 69) from '*high* pleasures' (l. 68) in life.

73.] Cf. the proverb, 'Diamonds cut diamonds'. Ferdinand seems to imply that any personal disaster is caused by our own individual natures or our human nature. However the rhyme draws attention to 'lust', and he might be aware that he is destroyed by incestuous desire for his sister, his *own dust*; in this sense, *we* is the royal plural in both lines of the couplet.

75–6. *I hold . . . me*] Bosola speaks as if the soul is leaving the body through the mouth—a common idea.

77. *pyramid*] a famed example of great labour in the service of pride.

85. *main*] chief part.

89. *rushes*] Green rushes were commonly strewed on the floors of apartments and on the stages of public theatres.

Pescara. How fatally, it seems, he did withstand
     His own rescue!
Malateste. [*To Bosola*] Thou wretched thing of blood,
     How came Antonio by his death?
Bosola. In a mist: I know not how—
     Such a mistake as I have often seen   95
     In a play. O, I am gone!
     We are only like dead walls, or vaulted graves,
     That, ruined, yields no echo. Fare you well.
     It may be pain, but no harm to me to die
     In so good a quarrel. O, this gloomy world!   100
     In what a shadow, or deep pit of darkness,
     Doth womanish and fearful mankind live!
     Let worthy minds ne'er stagger in distrust
     To suffer death or shame for what is just—
     Mine is another voyage.   [*Dies.*] 105
Pescara. The noble Delio, as I came to th' palace,
     Told me of Antonio's being here, and showed me
     A pretty gentleman, his son and heir.

               Enter DELIO [*with* Antonio's Son].

Malateste. O, sir, you come too late!
Delio.   I heard so, and
     Was armed for 't ere I came. Let us make noble use   110
     Of this great ruin, and join all our force
     To establish this young, hopeful gentleman
     In 's mother's right. These wretched eminent things
     Leave no more fame behind 'em than should one
     Fall in a frost, and leave his print in snow;   115
     As soon as the sun shines, it ever melts,
     Both form, and matter.—I have ever thought
     Nature doth nothing so great, for great men,
     As when she's pleased to make them lords of truth:
     Integrity of life is fame's best friend,   120
     Which nobly, beyond death, shall crown the end.   *Exeunt.*
                         FINIS.

---

     94. *mist*] Cf. IV.ii.187, and note.
     97. *dead*] continuous, unbroken; see V.ii.337, and note.
     103. *stagger in mistrust*] hesitate.
     120. Integrity] Among meanings current were 'wholeness', 'soundness',
freedom from moral corruption', and 'innocence, honesty, sincerity'.